THE MASTER ARCHITECT SERIES IV

DOMINIQUE PERRAULT

Selected and Current Works

THE MASTER ARCHITECT SERIES IV

DOMINIQUE PERRAULT

Selected and Current Works

First published in Australia in 2001 by
The Images Publishing Group Pty Ltd
ACN 059 734 431
6 Bastow Place, Mulgrave, Victoria 3170
Telephone (61 3) 9561 5544 Facsimile (61 3) 9561 4860

National Library of Australia Cataloguing-in-Publication data

Dominique Perrault: selected and current works.

Bibliography.
Includes index.
ISBN 1 86470 054 8.

1. Perrault, Dominique. 2 Architects – France.
3 Architecture, Modern – 20th century – France.
I. Perrault, Dominique. (Series: Master architect series IV.)

720.92

Edited by Andy Whyte
Designed by The Graphic Image Studio Pty Ltd,
Mulgrave, Australia

Printed in Hong Kong

Acknowledgments
Thank you to Dominique Perrault Studio: Natalie Plagaro Cowee
and Gaëlle Lauriot Prévost.

Photographs: Georges Fessy
                    Werner Hutmacher
                    André Morin
                    Perrault Projets
                    Gaëlle Lauriot-Prévost
                    Marie Clérin

Contents

Introduction

By Frederic Migayrou

Elementary dispositions Dominique Perrault's architecture is truly non-hierarchical; it avails itself of all the elements of an earlier architectonics and rearranges these according to a deliberately conceptual logic. A whole set of procedures, from the design to its realization, are thus overturned.

The architect seizes upon all the moments that make up the sequences leading to the conception and realization of a building – the process, that is – and makes the lasting material of an intervention from them.

Behind these skills, these decisions, the complex study and development of the idea, which define the architect as a creator, it is time itself that is undoubtedly the object of the architect's whole attention, his only preoccupation, the permanent restlessness of a present he tirelessly seeks to actualize. Indeed, what Perrault's architecture challenges is the idea of time that has formed the very essence of architectural culture, an idea that turns every building into a monument, a memory, an idea that founds, that historicizes, that would like architecture to possess an historical rationale, a truth. Dominique Perrault pleads for validity in architecture, he wants architecture to be effective, to be experienced by all, to have an instant rapport with each of us. It is Enlightenment reason he attacks, a reason that has fuelled classicism, and modernism too, a reason that seeks after rules and laws, a reason that seeks to determine the principles which legitimize and control architectural form. Dominique Perrault derives his main principles from praxis, from an ongoing research in which he endlessly reinvents the specificity of a space, of a form, of an intervention. For him, architecture is a constantly renewed activity, a consistently original act, a set of decisions that organize a unique situation. Architecture is no longer the result of a composition, but of a state of mind that calls equally on forms, materials and the abilities of all who participate in the elaboration of a project.

This implies, then, an architecture lacking in reference; neither modern nor postmodern, it functions with urgency, is immediate in nature and rejects history. It would therefore be illusory, when grasping, when trying to define Perrault's work, to seek models or analogies drawn from superficial comparison. Certain objects are present, but one can no longer speak of forms, and the cubes and parallelepipeds common in much of his work are only *a priori* devices; they are the outcomes of transitory conventions, differing states of stabilization, of the management of a permanently mutating situation. Given its lack of syntax, of obvious linguistic elements, we cannot easily scrutinize his architecture for principles or referential images, such as a particular "Miesian" use of glass, or certain spatial organizations borrowed from Louis I. Kahn, which critics must have been quick to point to. Architectural culture does not possess here ineluctable authority, it has no set method; instead it is a material, a resource, a tool like any other. Dominique Perrault insists on an architecture without style, without expressions, which does not entail definition, the precedence of any language. His work does not respond to a constant syntax, applicable according to the appropriateness of the situation, the program; it is not organized as an aesthetic project that holds knowledge, norms, a morality of practice in check. The project's definition is a direct consequence of the context, of the determining factors present in it, which are analysed, put forward as a resource, a particular richness, which must be interpreted by means of the tools of architecture, and thus transfigured, reconverted.

For him, context means, literally, "with the text" – to supplement what already appears to make sense, or to reveal what is not immediately legible, the lines of force of a landscape barely perceptible on an open expanse of ground or in a destructured environment, spatial organizations that must be revalued.

Dominique Perrault's conceptualism is not historicist, he does not dwell on the memory of a place, of an extant building; he is tectonic, he takes physical hold of the territory. To dig beneath a small chateau to house the **Usinor-Sacilor Conference Center** (1991), and to place the chateau on a mirror surface that reflects back this architecture of representation, is to deny this arrogant play with inscription and representation that nourished 19th-century architecture; it is to nullify the play of historical reference and to retain merely the slightly antiquated image of a building whose volume is exceeded by the program it now hosts. The traditional diagnosis of usage and function is only one of the aspects of the work, which is henceforth also built around an environmental analysis of defined or defining areas. The sum of elements that define and organize the specificity of a site – its history, social usage, its topography – are assimilated to a force field which, in order to optimize its use and management, the architect addresses in its entirety. The lines of force organizing the territory are defined in this way, as is splendidly demonstrated in the model for the **Redevelopment of the Ile Sainte-Anne in Nantes** (1994), in which raw materials applied to an aerial view of the site generate lines of tension, vectors and zones capable of articulating and redefining the economy of this particular territory. In opposition to a sociological reading, which looks for traces of the sedimentation of human praxis in the city or the territory, Perrault strives to be a geographer or a geologist; he rejects the authority of a past age, of an external time, of history, and retains only its current, active elements. Space does not possess its own ontology; for Perrault there is no antecedent, essence or primary nature that would rule over the built domain and that would have to be opposed to human praxis. There are, argues Perrault, "different natures, extending from the most virgin to the most artificial, natures which coexist in a simultaneous whole." This materialism, this veritable physicalism, redefines the world as a complexity in which man rediscovers his capacity for definition, for intervention.

Nature is no longer the domain of indeterminacy, it asserts itself as an object of knowledge, it is submitted to the laws of regulation and industrial production, it is exploited, exhausted in the extreme, but it is also available for mastering anew; nature can be developed, it is the object of specific study and development.

To cultivate nature is to produce it, it is to avail ourselves of all the various kinds of knowledge we have at our disposal to induce it, to supplement it, to energetically endow it with a syntactical potential that is central to architectural language. And so Perrault conceives a hanging-garden-like forest for the **International Port Terminal in Yokohama** (1994); he makes the **Kansai-Kan Library** (1996 competition) disappear into the earth of a landscaped park; and, of course, he inscribes an inaccessible pine forest at the center of the **Bibliothèque Nationale de France in Paris** (1989–95). Behind the apparent violence or arbitrariness of these interventions, an actual mutation in the relationship between nature and architecture articulates the logic of design. If vegetation has long been the object of human engineering – a fiction of natural order within the classical garden – the idea of the park, the forest, requires the architect of today to call on all the technical dimensions of an understanding of the environment in order to go beyond the still-formalist logics of landscapism. When Dominique Perrault proposes such a brutalist use of nature, he does so to allow its phenomenal and sentient force to freely express itself, contra any overly cultural or architectural understanding of the garden, of green space. It is the landscape as a whole that is under scrutiny, that is saved from the endless temptations of planning. Architecture must not take possession of space; it no longer defines the measure of a geometric order. Instead, it must use every means at its disposal to remain aloof from spatial hierarchies and to yield to the possibilities of simultaneous action. The architect must, according to Dominique Perrault, generate the effects of spatiality; he must, by using simple gestures, create an order that rejects all mediation, a unique and immediate layout that does not strive to be a system, an organizing principle. Space must be concretely apprehended, brought into being according to a factual system, a unique, open-ended experience. Architecture must stick to this economy of layout, in which space is defined through the sort of simple intervention Dominique Perrault has endlessly proposed: incrusting, weaving, enclosing, engraving, installing, anchoring, sectioning, blending, splicing, extending, flooding, concealing.

Is there a Dominique Perrault minimalism? Can we really define a minimalist architectural aesthetic long after the critical success of this art movement in the USA? The analytical contrivances of a spatial definition based on the disposition of primary elements, as seen in the works of Walter de Maria or Richard Long, are widely deployed in many projects in order to attain an urban scale. The architectural object is reaffirmed as an element that gives space a direction, as a vector that renders the spectator conscious of a space that once seemed transparent to him, unquestioned evidence of the wide expanse. The building-as-object is reduced to a function by which it is all but refuted; it is a device of disposition, it is generic to an actualization of the site. This reduction is not, however, the effect of a kind of purism or of a simple economy of means aimed at reducing architectural language, analogous to Mies van der Rohe's famous "less is more." Space is no longer just this simple possibility, the final, modern form of Miesian space organized, as Beatriz Colomina once noted, by a gaze turned towards a horizon completely permeated by transparency. In contradistinction to the modern space of the *tabula rasa*, there is no spatial precedence, no pure, virgin space, no infinite white expanse – minimalism for Perrault means that there is no *a priori*, given space.

Minimalism, here, does not stand for a reduction of means, but rather an amplification of means that have their starting point in a reduced syntax.

Any project will begin with a pragmatic investigation into how to understand the territory, and the layout of elements forming a spatial field will lead, as often happens in the case of Carl Andre,

to a displacement of spatial tension. The architect tries to induce a physicality that has to be experienced, by simultaneously appealing to an individual perception that has constitutional value and, more universally, to urban scale. It is the active dimension of this minimalist perspective that will dominate an architecture that appears, more and more, like an architecture having its legitimization in the intervention. Circle and square, as in the **Berlin Velodrome and Olympic Swimming Pool** (1992–98), give material form to these combined investigations, in which layout is ordained as a principle, the intersection of an idea and a location, the moment when concept and context coincide, as Dominique Perrault himself put it (**Exhibition at the Galerie Denise Rene**, 1991). Struts that cross each other and brace a walkway guide the design for the **Charles de Gaulle Bridge** (1988). A sheet of lead tied to a surface becomes an allegory of the relationship between the building and the ground it is on. An object–concept, the conception of an object, the layout frees architecture from the design, the plan; it organizes the territory in an order born of practice, of shared experience. The plan is not a previously defined field, and this once more calls into question a practice of spatial organization and the architectural vocabulary it supports: distribution, composition, hierarchization... The notion of plans leads to the idea of a potential inscription that is itself accompanied by words like "insertion", "limit", "foundation", "opening" – words that denote an almost ideological vision of surface. Architecture is, in fact, an art of separation. It delimits, circumscribes, raises walls which define and constrain the architectural object. If Mies van der Rohe fulfilled the very idea of separation by transfiguring it into a wall of glass, Perrault goes as far as to deny the very idea of the window; a refusal of the idea of opening as a compositional element, in which the relationship between inside and outside is rejected. Not the least of the paradoxes of this so-called minimal architecture is to invert the logic of the curtain-wall, to repudiate a metaphysics of separation that still claims absolute transparency. The entire syntax of a relationship to the plan, the surface, implodes, beneath the blows of this open logic of layout. The wall is therefore rejected in favor of the enclosure, the medieval square plan of the **Bibliothèque Nationale de France** (1989–95), the suspended structures of the **Wilhelmgalerie** (1993), the design of the **Grande Stade in Melun-Senart** (1993). The arbitrary enclosure, a squaring of the design, freed from the constraints of the economy of the plan, creates an incredible feeling of openness. The ground is no longer an obstacle, a frontier, a limit it itself; it is part of the program and is no longer left as the mere underpinning of the foundations. Dominique Perrault does not hesitate to involve it in the majority of his projects (the **Angers Universite de Lettres et de Droit**, 1986), to merge the built object into the ground, leaving only a trace of it on the surface, like the almost graphic stigmata of the circle and square of the Berlin Velodrome and Olympic Swimming Pool (1992–98). As the **Hotel Industriel Jean-Baptiste Berlier** (1986–91) shows, the floors are storage shelves on which people or objects are placed, on which different functional elements are moved around, and which no longer refer to a particular level, to a functional hierarchy.

Without walls the box has a merely conventional value, it is an enclosure, it protects a territory, it forms a refuge; it is also an *enceinte* which, protected by an envelope that permanently gives onto the world, has an almost matricial function. This rejection of dividing walls gives rise to a new kind of curtain, a veiling materialized in the insistent use of metal mesh, or by means of the effective transparency of a sheet of glass, rapidly concealed by a second screen layer. Again paradoxically, Dominique Perrault insists on the use of grids which, liberated from the plan, from the control of perspectival projections, become a conventional device, a simple pattern that no longer refers to the idea of an external spatial continuum. The grid creates a regular area that can be articulated on top of another; it is merely the layout tool, it is a moment's activity, an affirmation that is, of course, subject to scrutiny, to change, to distortion, to making way for some other kind of organizing principle. Facades, floors, partitions – the grid is an ineludible syntactic element in Dominique Perrault's work, which, for all that, has no structural value; it remains a raw element, exactly like the material itself, it has just as much formal as material value. The actual status of the materials must change; they no longer have syntactic value in their own right, along the lines of glass or brick. The material is form and matter at one and the same time, wood, greenery, metal mesh; it attains a specific qualifying potential, it is valued for its phenomenality, be it raw matter or industrial texture. The whole hierarchy of construction is overturned, procedures and usages becoming interchangeable. Nature is an object of engineering that can be chosen at will among endless possibilities, in order, perhaps, to render its effects more natural. High-precision technological materials can equally as well be used for their symbolic charge, for the phenomenal and emotional effects they convey. Vegetation granted object-status; industrial materials will be instead naturalized to the extreme. A phenomenon of general translatability; nature and the industrial world interpenetrate, everything is legible in terms of accumulated procedures, of serviceability, nothing is frightening any more, there are no more deprived areas, peripheries, wastelands, there is only a state of things. Dominique Perrault takes the idea of flexibility to its limit by assuming the world of industrial production to be a physical domain.

In a word, Perrault's oeuvre is without style, without expression, it does not encumber itself with any affectation, any code or presupposed knowledge. It invites a sort of unknowing, a refusal of any supposed meaning, of architecture as a defining principle. Dominique Perrault runs the idea of meaning in architecture to ground; within a very French tradition, he argues for the boundaries of a metaphysics in which architecture must accept the principle of its own disappearance. The gesture is not new; the end of humankind, the end of philosophy, the end of history – years ago structuralism had already made declarations of this kind familiar to us. What he dissimulates is the refusal of typologies, of

a pre-existing language that could be applied to any definition of space. His minimalism does not lead to the phenomenal truth of a purer space being elaborated from a new purism that balances light and materials. Perrault's architecture strikes at the very heart of a structuralist vision of creation that presupposed the permanent equivalence, traducible in linguistic terms, of the means the architect has, a syntactic understanding that had swamped all the debates between moderns and postmoderns in the tumultuous questioning of meaning and expression. Dominique Perrault dismisses this quest for architectural truth, this historicism of the postmoderns, this yielding to a phenomenology of modernism with its Heideggerian overtones, by challenging current appeals to certain principles of authority. There is no subjectivism remaining in the background any more, no subject of history or of expression, be that subject collective or individual; architecture can no longer maintain its authority through intentional distance. Turning to Maurice Blanchot, Perrault speaks of blank writing, takes architecture beyond the traditional realms of expression. He confirms himself to the founding event of an architectural "there is." This claim immediately takes on a political connotation, the end of the profession, of the architect; the discipline must be practiced without distance, without limits; it resides in the displacements of identity between monumental and human, self-publicity and intimacy, between city and nature. "Nothing," the text in which Perrault attempts to rediscover a primary phenomenal meaning to architecture, and in which the body and emotion are established as modes of experiencing and understanding space, has not simply a passive dimension.

Perrault's conceptualism is no longer simply analytical and critical; it has an operative function, it deems disposition to be an authentic constructive principle. By neutralizing architecture, dominique perrault invents a path leading to proximity in the architect's work, an architecture in act, a manifest architecture of the neutral.

SELECTED AND CURRENT WORKS

Bibliothèque nationale de France

Design/Completion 1989/1995, winning competition project
Quai Francois Mauriac, 75013 Paris, France
Client: Ministry of Culture, Department for Public Buildings, and Institute
of the Bibliothèque nationale de France
Mies Van der Rohe European Prize of Architecture 1997
Surface: 350,000 m²
Cost: 3,500,000,000 FF (1989 value, before charges and taxes)

A place, not a building

The *grands projets* of President of the
Republic Francois Mitterrand are all
closely associated with a site and a history –
in short, a place with a name. The
Bibliothèque nationale de France is built
on a stretch of industrial wasteland on the
banks of the Seine in the East End of Paris.
It represents the starting point for a
complete restructuring of this entire sector
of the 13th *arrondissement*. The institution
encompasses within it an element of
grandeur and an element of generosity.
If we refer ourselves to the urban history
of the great monuments that have been
fundamental signs of the city's thrust
toward new territory, the greatest fit that
it is possible to give to Paris consist, today,
in offering space, and emptiness – a place
that is open, free, and stirring.
Accordingly, the enormous building,
envisaged as a demonstration of
architectural emphasis and affectation,
is transformed into a piece of work on
the void – an absolute luxury in the city –
proposing to the history of France a focus
on immateriality and non-ostentation. It is
this context that engendered the concept
of the project.

Continued

1

Engineering Consultants:
Perrault Associés S.A., Séchaud & Bossuyt, H.G.M.
Guy Huguet S.A., Syseca, Technip Seri Construction,
Pieffet-Corbin-Tomasina, A.C.V, Sauveterre
Program: Working and reading rooms for 4000
readers, reception and public services, stockrooms,
400 km of shelves, 20 million books,
administration, plantrooms, auditoriums,
restaurants, exhibition rooms,
and 700 parking places

1   The library towers above the Salpetière hospital of
Paris, 13ème
Opposite:
Lateral access

A square for Paris, a library for France

An initiatory place and not some monster of a building, part temple and part supermarket. A place of reference for the East End of Paris. A place that is part and parcel of the continuity of the sequence of large empty spaces along the Seine, like the Place de la Concorde, the Champ de Mars, and the Invalides. In this way, the site beside the Seine becomes one of major importance with the activation of this place. In an operation designed to save and redeem the place, the institution introduces its generosity, while the Bibliothèque nationale de France contributes its influence and radiance. With this combination of a free and open space, built to the scale of the capital, and horizontality, the Bibliothèque nationale de France unfurls its breadth and volume by way of its four "beacon-like" markers, akin to tension-rods or braces for the flat area between them, offering a verticality that defines a virtual volume, which, in turn, crystallizes all the magic, presence and poetry of the complex.

Continued

3

3   Belvedere over the core forest, entrance to the
    Bibliothèque nationale
4   Cloister façade
5   View of research halls from the garden

4

5

6

6   View from the surrounding buildings
7   One of the four access ways to the esplanade
8   Descent towards the library

A symbolic place

With its four corner towers resembling four open books, all facing one another, and delimiting a symbolic place, the Bibliothèque nationale de France – a mythical place – imposes its presence and identity on the scale of the city by the adjustment of its four corners. These urban landmarks develop and enhance the idea of the "book" with a random occupation of the towers, which present themselves like an accumulation of learning, of knowledge that is never complete, and of a slow but ongoing process of sedimentation. Other complementary metaphors spring to mind, be they book-towers, or silos, or vast racks with countless shelves, or vertical labyrinths, and all these unambiguous images converge on a powerful identity of these architectural objects. The establishment of an open square underpins the notion of availability, as applied to treasure. It is the towers that have helped to situate and identify this treasure as cultural. The public space will offer a direct and natural physical contact between the sacred institution and the person in the street. The inclusion of an "inlaid", sunken garden rounds off the symbolic siting of the project, offering a quiet spot away from the fuss and bother of the city. Like a cloister, this tranquil, unruffled space will invite contemplation and a flowering of intellectual endeavour.

Continued

7

8

9

10

11

9   Fire exit from secondary patio,
      "longitudinal garden"

10   Fire staircase and tower façade

11   Mobile interior sun shelters for the
      office levels of the towers

12

A magic place

This project is a piece of art, a minimalist installation, the "less is more" of emotion, where objects and the materials of which they are made count for nothing without the light which transcends them. Towers, case- or sheath-like structures of glass, with a double skin and sun filters that multiply the reflections and magnify the shadows; the absolute magic of the diffraction of light by means of these crystalline prisms. Nature offset, with a garden where all one sees is the foliage of the trees. "A sea of trees, a froth of leaves". In short, the soft protection of undergrowth, with its aromas and rustling sounds; reunions with oneself, and with another world. Night vision: the Bibliothèque nationale de France is set in a halo of light, emanating from the garden and the service periphery. A diaphanous light rises up through the interiors of the glass towers, culminating in the four topmost points, which shimmer like four lighthouse beacons. This liquid spreads over the square, while the towers are reflected in the Seine.

Continued

12&13   The forest core: winter 1994

13

An urban place

What could be more urban and more public than a pedestrian square? The challenge of creating a void preserves the future of the district, while at the same time steering its development and offering conspicuous architectural requirements, such as can be learnt from the great squares of Paris. A square is a space that is lined or hemmed; a system of continuous structures – combining porches, covered walks, and a cornice height forming a skyline – delimits the public place. This setting acts as a backdrop, not a waterfront foreground. It accommodates diverse and varied architectural scripts, the sole rule being their shared role of accompanying, in their own right, the institution's urban influence.

14   The forest core
15   Walkway around treetops at upper peristyle
       (entrance level)

15

16

16 Main entrance hall
17 Escalator lobby hung as entrance to the research
reading rooms

17

18

18&19   Lower peristyle walkway around the
        forest core, access to the research
        reading rooms
  20   Access to lecture hall

19

21

21 Indirect lighting, camera and loudspeaker
22 Metal mesh sun filter on public reading room
Following pages:
   Research reading room

22

24

24 Research reading room and overview of
    individual lecture rooms
25 Research reading room

25

27

26&27   Research reading room

28

28 Research reading rooms with the cloister forest
in the background
Opposite:
Public reading rooms with a metal mesh light
filter over the "longitudinal garden"

31

30   Research reading rooms
31   Detail of the fibre optic lamp

32

33

32&33   Furniture study: design by Dominique Perrault
         and Gaëlle Lauriot-Prévost
Opposite:
         Research reading room

Eur Convention Center

Design Competition 1998
Eur Centro, Rome, Italy
Client: City of Rome
Surface: 55,000 m²
Program: Principal exhibition hall (10,000 people), 3 small exhibition halls (100–300 people), restaurants, cafes, commercial center and shops, offices, independent auditorium and hall (2,000 people), and parking

The Convention Center in Rome is like the honeycomb of a huge beehive – a place of intense activity on all floors, day and night.

The building is a pure volume, simple and minimal in form: a rectangular prism, a "glass box" pierced at its center by an enormous balcony–loggia overlooking the city. A piazza in front of this opens onto the avenue. From the piazza one can reach the loggia at the center of the building via a series of grand staircases; yet one can also reach the exhibition hall directly from the street level and, via the side entrances, the congress center and its auditorium.

The different functions are assembled and connected along the side streets or "cheeks" of the building. The horizontal and vertical circulation systems extend throughout the length and height of these streets. This side structure, located between the city and the center as a kind of INTERFACE, provides for adaptation and flexibility of use in both time and space.

The different parts can thereby function independently of each other. They are presented as freestanding platforms, with a ceiling height of around 9 meters. They can be used in their totality, or only in part.

This "glass box" is vibrant and alive with movement and light; this INNER LIFE is the "material" of the facade – reflections, transparencies, brilliance, clarity. The prism, heavy or lightweight according to the lighting and the point of view, changes and metamorphoses throughout the day and night.

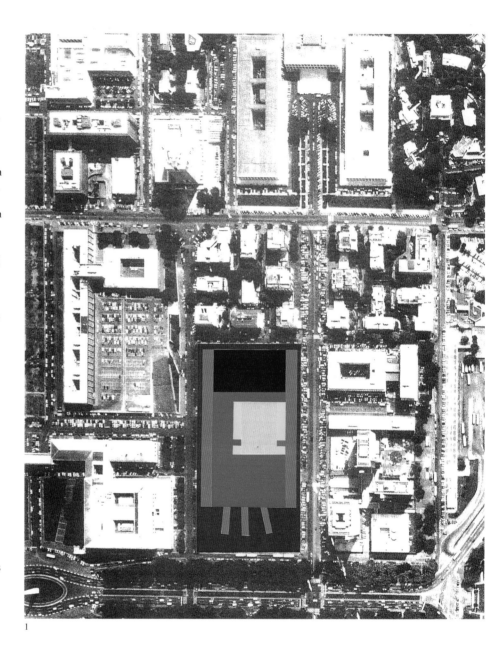

1

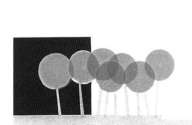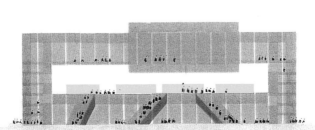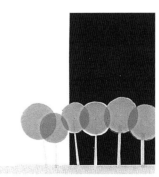

2

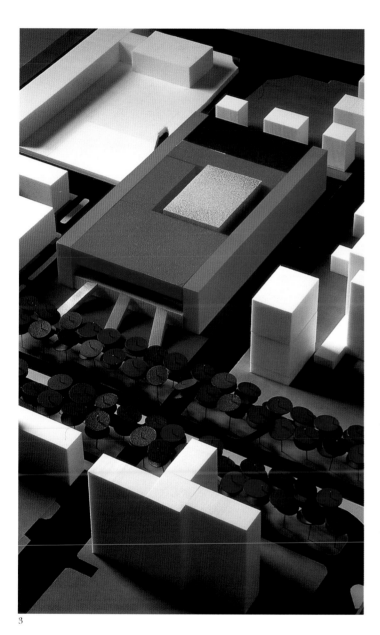

3

4

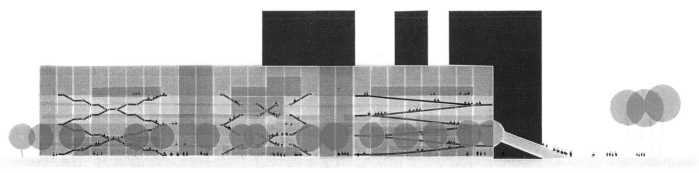

5

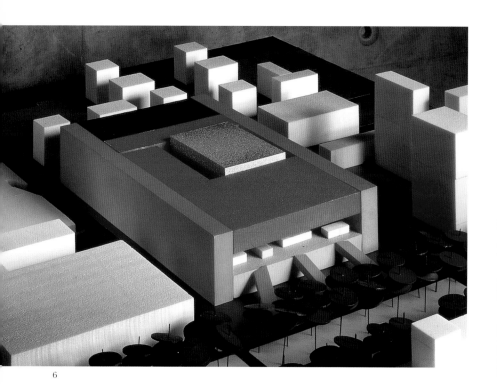

6

7

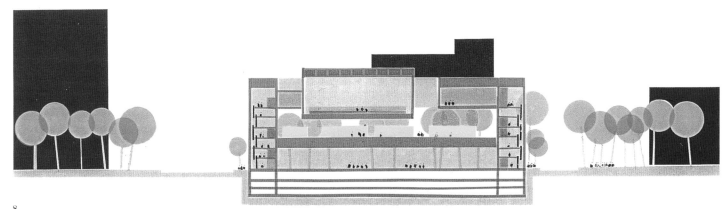

8

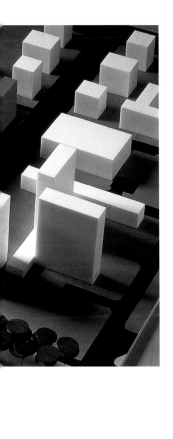

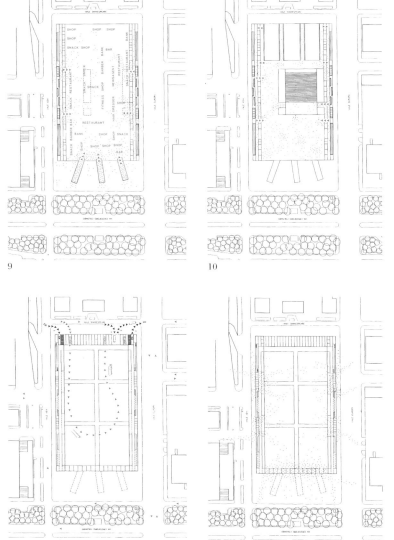

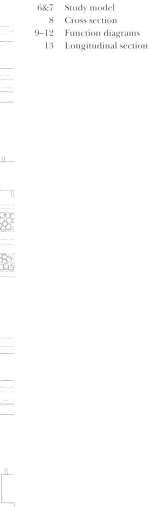

9

10

11

12

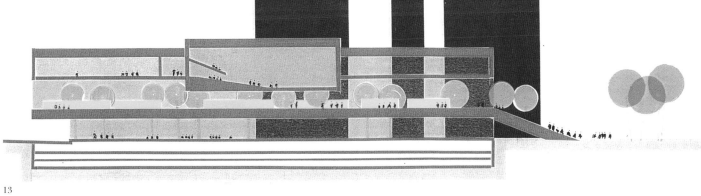

13

Redevelopment of the Falck Site

Design Competition 1998, competition project
Centre of Sesto San Giovanni (north of Milan), Italy
Client: City of Sesto San Giovanni, County of Milan, Groupe Falck
1,320,139 m² (total area): raw soil area 633,934 m²
(green spaces 525,210 m²), and circulation network
Program: To the north of Milan, on the remains of a huge industrial site, at the center of an emerging urban neighborhood, and along the edge of a long and winding planned "green corridor," it seemed right to create an adjoining "green space", half-urban, half-natural, and modern – that is, without reference to earlier centuries – linking order and disorder, rigor and fantasy, simplicity and exuberance.

The idea of the project is to give birth/semblance to a park at the heart of the town. That is to say, to develop the town and its streets, avenues, blocks, squares and gardens so as to reunite the southern neighborhoods with those in the north, the east with the west; in a word, TO WEAVE NEW LINKS/RELATIONS between the different districts. The natural layout of this park makes no reference to French, Italian or English-style gardens. This garden is an act of LAND ART, an act of contemporary art which considers the history of the site and its industrial context as a source of "building material" for the conception of a park specific to Sesto San Giovanni. Nature as a material forming the architecture of a town is not a new idea, but NATURE CONSIDERED AS AN INDUSTRIAL ELEMENT, as in the aeroplane, locomotive and other engine parts formerly manufactured in the Falck factories, that is something new, something rich in historical resonance, yet also up-to-date and even forward-looking.

1

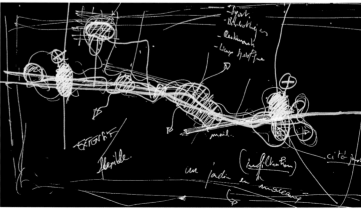

2

1　"Plan-relief" model
2　Sketch
3　Site plan

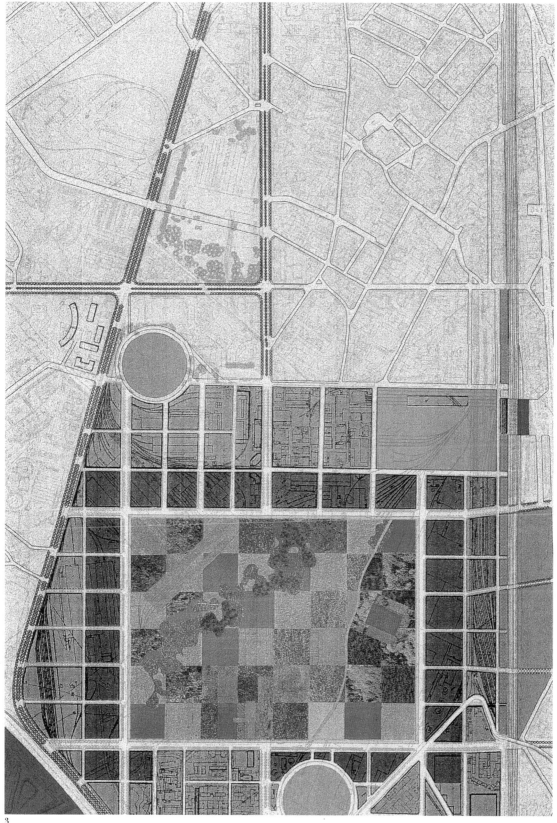

3

This binary grid, akin to a chessboard – with its 95 ¥ 95 meter squares – permits the setting up of a supple, open and flexible system of realization. It is constructed square by square, respecting certain traces on the ground, or certain fine trees, or certain industrial buildings for their structure or their volume. It is necessary to "give time to time." Step by step, square after square, the town is built, the park laid out, with no *a priori* aesthetic as to style, just a basic geometry, measure, and reading, so as NOT TO LOSE ANYTHING of the existing context, WHILE TRANSFORMING IT INTO A NEW PART OF TOWN, rich in urban diversity.

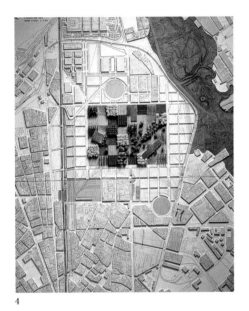

4

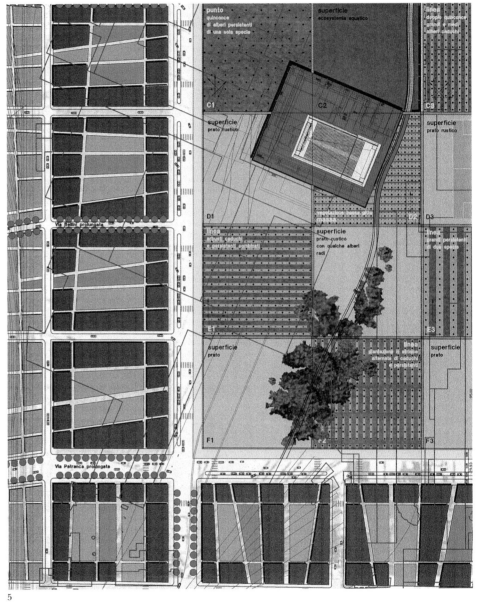

5

4   "Plan-relief" model
5   Planning detail
6–9   Landscaping pattern book:
     6 Point
     7 Line
     8 Mass
     9 Plain

6

7

8

9

Pfleiderer Stand

Design 1999
Bau 99, Munich.
Client: Pfleiderer
Consulting Engineer: Guy Morisseau
Surface: 5 m²

Design of the Pfleiderer stand at the
Construction annual Hall of Munich.
The use of new technologies and of the
company's products was a must in the
conception of the design. Therefore, it was
the construction of a door out of a metal
mesh which was innovative. Nevertheless,
the wooden chassis and the use of mineral
wool inside the door were standard
production elements.

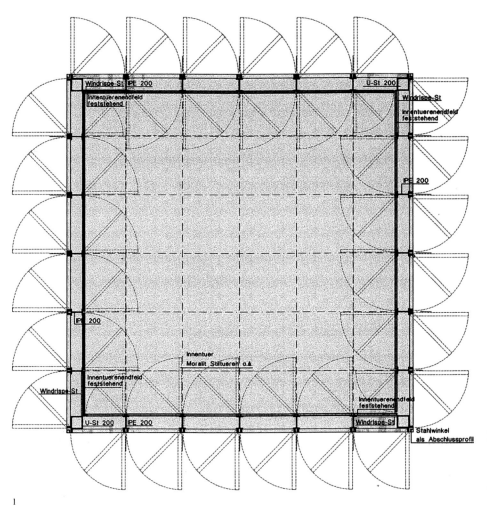

1

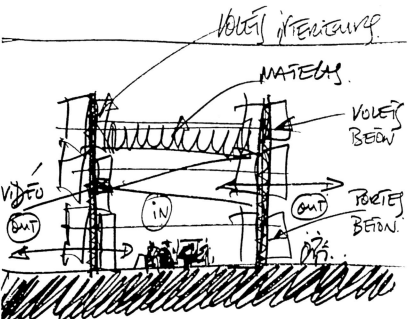

2

1 Plan
2 Sketch
3 Elevation
4&5 Presentation model

3

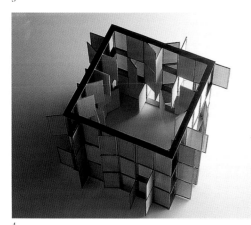

4

5

Temple of Mitra

Design 1998, on direct command of the City Hall, competition project
Historic Centre of Naples, Italy
Client: City of Naples, Italy
Surface: Hanging gardens 1,000 m², archeological excavations 1,000 m²
Program: Landscape design for the historic monument to reinforce
the value of the Mitra Temple and to increase the number of visitors

In the heart of Naples, the population density is greater than that in Hong Kong. In the heart of Naples, sedimentation of the layers of history has been effected by the telluric alchemy of this area of the globe.

In the heart of Naples, the blood of the people is mixed with the blood of volcanoes. Noise, smell, heat, topography, and movement are so many ingredients of a Neapolitan character that only finds respite in the presence of an exuberant nature. The Temple of Mitra, an open-air ruin stuck at the end of a canyon of over-inhabited buildings, is a stopover in time. This mark in the ground, this imprint of history, this trace of flamboyant mythology, sizzles beneath the never-ending heat of the Neapolitan city.

The design for a hanging garden, suspended between earth and sky as if torn from the geological crust, offers a moment of calm and repose in this pullulating

1

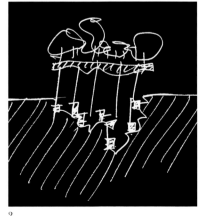

2

3

1   Section
2   Concept sketch
3   Study model
4   Urban approach

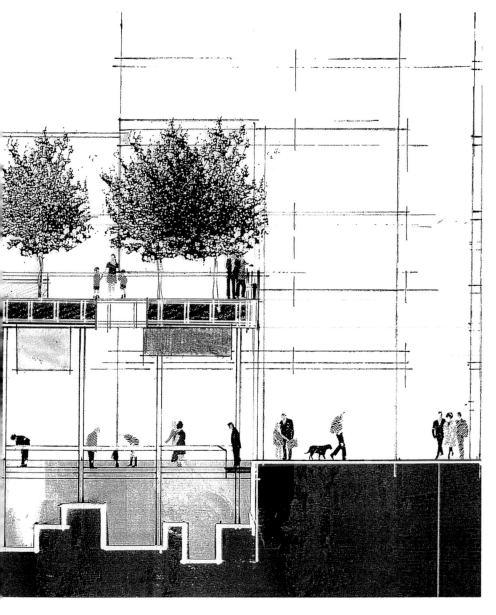

neighborhood. Such a poetic and violent telluric gesture permits matter to be extricated from itself. To emerge from its geological layer, let its entrails be glimpsed as if they were some didactic section, thus showing that Naples is a deep city.

A bit of nature, floating free, raised on a terrace by a rootlike bunch of metal pins; such is this Garden of Babylon planted in the heart of the melted stone.

And so the temple appears below, empty, expressing its mystery without, for all that, offering any explanation.

It will be necessary to penetrate inside, bury oneself there while discovering its innermost recesses – which will be the sole indications of a slow and defunct history. That is what this architectural project reveals by means of geological section; a place's history in the shape of Neapolitan ice-cream.

4

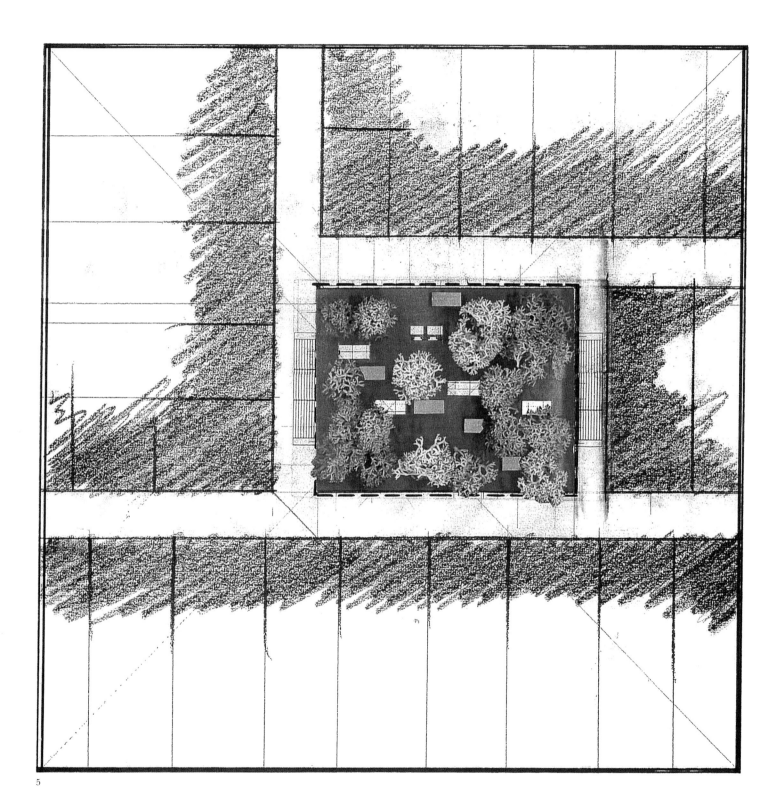

5

5   Ground floor
6   Study model
7   Level of the ruins

6

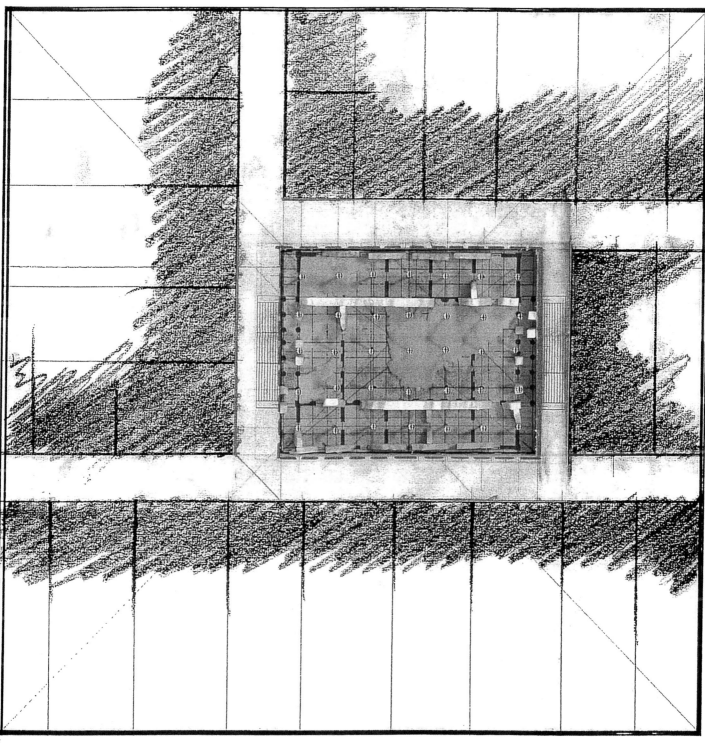

7

Installation Project for Francis Giacobetti's Work
HYMN

Design 1995, on direct command of the
Francis Giacobetti Cultural Association
Seine Banks, at the level of the Bibliothèque nationale de France,
Paris, France
Client: Francis Giacobetti Cultural Association
Surface: Sensitive plate/kaleidoscope 400 m²,
exposition space 750 m², technical space 400 m²
Program: Presentation of the photographic work HYMN by
Francis Giacobetti

The project is an "installation" in the contemporary art sense of the term; that is, an intervention based on the placement of an object in relation to its environment. Without "touching" the environment, the presence of this "sensitive plate" organizes a place by endowing it with its particular symbolic "meaning".

Francis Giacobetti's HYMN is rendered in perspective, multiplied to infinity, so true is it that the intellect is varied, multiform and incommensurable; the intellect is "a bit of sky fallen to earth," hurled down from on high, embedded in the ground but still luminous, lightweight and immaterial. This plate, vibrant with a thousand eyes (gazes), a thousand reflections, possessed of a thousand faces and rummaged through by a thousand hands, is the scheme for a magic and mythical place beside the Seine and at the foot of a monument subsuming all of human knowledge. The plate consists of glass panels containing a layer of liquid crystals (the image) activated by a low-voltage electrical signal. The plate is placed on slim steel columns, which modulate the exhibition space.

The upper level of the plate is flush with the embankment. Four moveable metal footbridges are placed above the glass, and cross over the plate and ponds. The itinerary at this level can be modified by moving the footbridges along the axis of the plate.

Metal stairways lead to the entrance to the exhibition space, which is four meters below the level of the embankment.

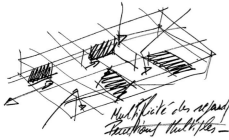

1

2

58

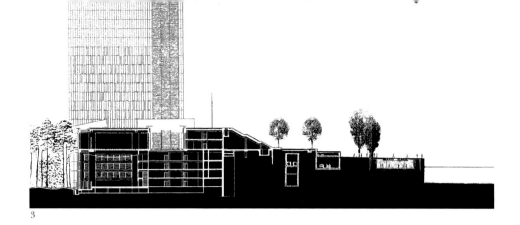

1 Sketch
2 Perspective over the sensitive plate
3 Cross section of the site between the Bibliothèque nationale de France and the river Seine

3

4

Inside, the walls and floor are of rough concrete (in contrast to the plate, a lightweight precision object). The walls have built-in projection screens for films and images.

The floor directly below the plate is divided up into concrete slabs sensitive to the movements of the visitor. Each slab is linked electronically to a cell in the plate. The visitor activates a cell through his or her own weight, thus triggering a three-part series of images. Seen from above, the plate becomes an object full of moving images, the three-part series being activated and deactivated, according to the rhythm of the movements below.

4   Perspective of the interior of the sensitive plate
5   Perspective under the sensitive plate
6   Cross section

5

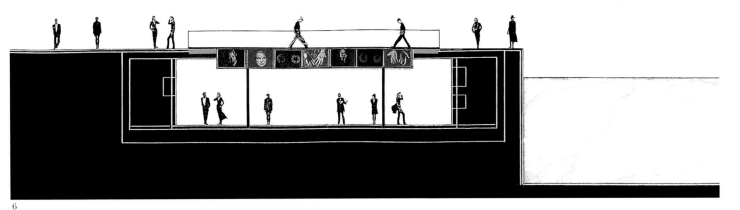

6

Montigalà Sports Complex

Design/Completion 1998/2002
Badalona, Barcelona Metropolitan Area, Spain
Client: Town of Badalona
Surface: 10 ha (total area): sport facilities, 50,000 m²
Architect's Mission: Urban and landscape studies; detailed design of sports facilities
Architect's Activities: Project for general urban development of Batlloria Valley. Town and landscape planning, insertion of a sports facilities complex
Program: 8,000-seat stadium, training fields 40,000 m², (constructed 2,000 m²), sports hall (swimming pool, basketball court, fitness equipment, 10,000 m²), and an additional soccer field for local teams

Between sea and mountain

In the midst of the peripheral development of a large town, a valley, the vestige of a natural landscape, appears to have been forgotten, and has thus been spared the rapid urbanization. At Montigalà, shopping centers are still springing up along the motorway, while a second motorway cuts the town in two, distancing a part of the city from the sea.

One could say that this valley is situated between sea and mountain. In fact it is located between two motorways, forming a visual link between sea and mountain, and an urban link between two parts of the town.

The idea of protecting this valley as a natural, open space, by giving it over to sporting activities, provides a positive use for the neighboring areas and allows for the creation of a landscape in which nature and architecture blend as one.

The project proposed a series of sequences, the more urban and "dense" to the south (the sea) giving way to the more landscape-like and "empty" to the north (the mountains).

1

1   View of the stadium and training field
2   Plan of the football stadium
3   Overall view of the site

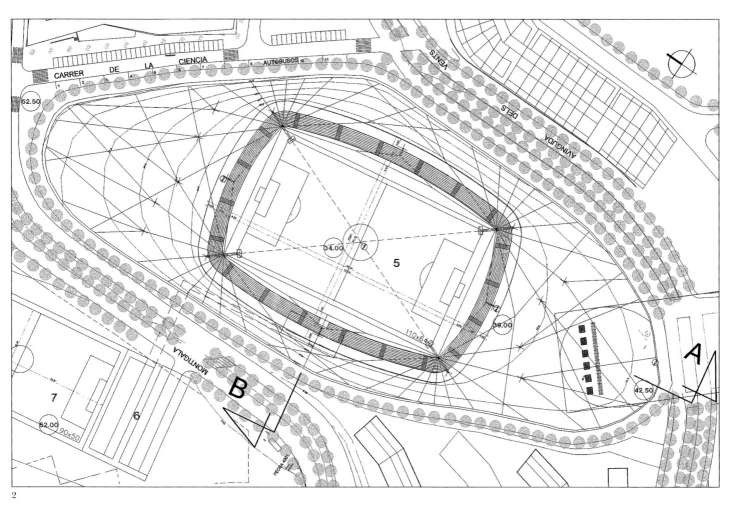

2

3

We defined four sequences:

- sports facilities for the adjacent neighborhoods and parking spaces, organized "as in town";

- the football stadium, which accommodates sporting and festive events;

- the training ground, which accompanies the central sports facility and forms the entrance to the leisure and sports park; and

- the leisure and sports park, which extends the network of sports facilities and provides for a less professional and more "poetic" practising of sport.

These four parts of the valley house a wide diversity of facilities, which link up like the beads of a rosary to form a "network".

4

4 Site plan and section
5 Study simulation of metal cover structure
6 Sketch

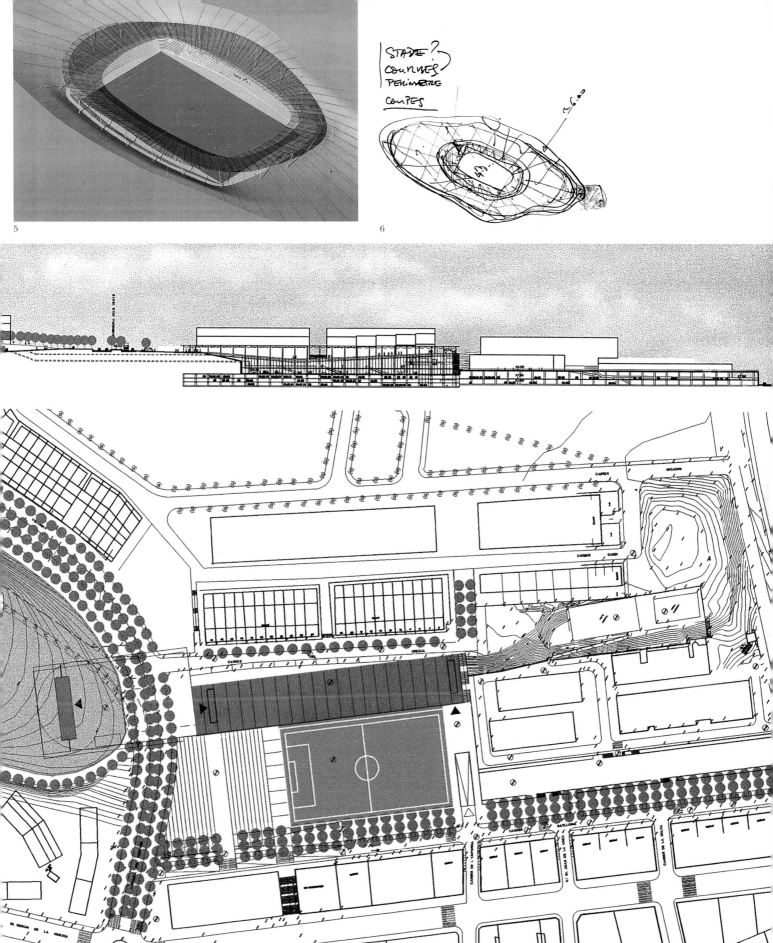

5

6

The whole project is organized along an avenue extending from the "lower" ("downtown") motorway to the "upper" ("uptown") motorway, considering that the topography of the valley guides and orients the urbanization of this city fragment.

The avenue assumes various forms, depending on the context: it is urban, in the form of a mall, in the denser part; it will become a path or lane where it crosses the sports park.

This variation on a theme, progressing from the more urban to the more landscape-like, provides a varied and multifarious set of responses *vis-à-vis* the urban quality of spaces, the design of streets, the construction of public facilities, places for community life, and the quality – and protection – of the environment, and attempts to respect the inhabitants of the adjoining neighborhoods and their ways of life. The project foregrounds the geography of the site and introduces, in the very heart of the territory, the founding acts of a new development, such as the football stadium built in a crater, or by following the forms of the valley, fading into the landscape and allowing only its shading net to emerge, like some nomad's tent pitched there.

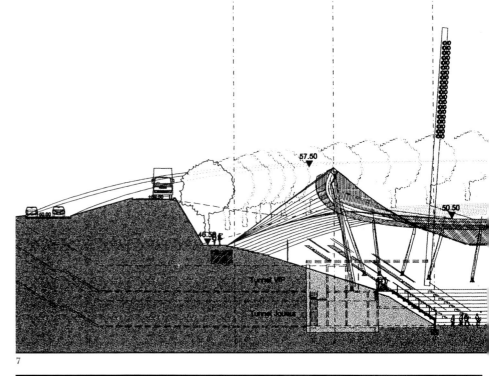

7

8

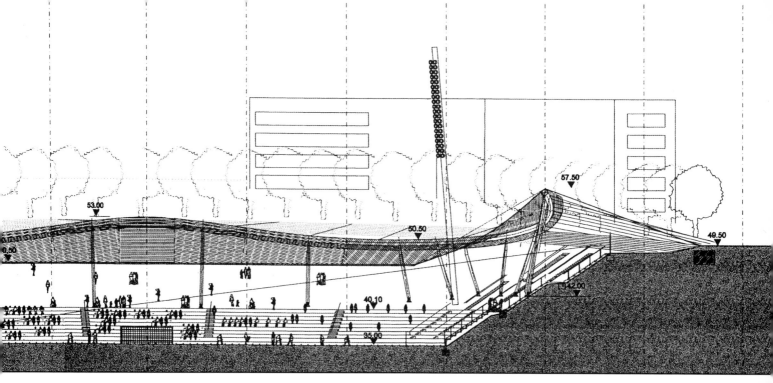

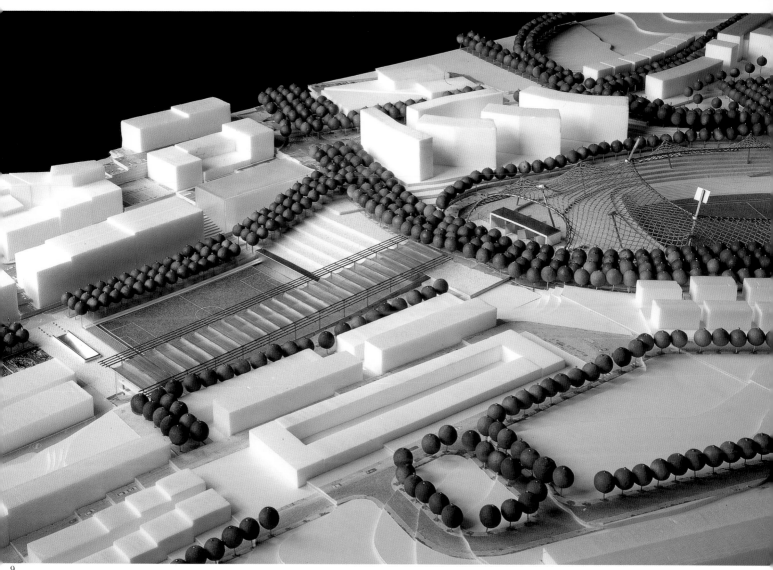

7 Longitudinal section through the stadium
8 Entrance detail
9 Complementary sport services and training field

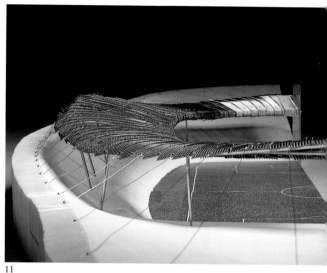

11

Left:
Main stadium simulation
11   Study model for the structure of the metal mesh cover

Lehrter Bahnhof Tower

Design Competition 1998, competition project–winner
Lehrter Bahnhof, Berlin, Germany
Client: Tishman Speyer Properties, Germany
Surface: 50,000 m²
Program: Conception of a tower with offices, a commercial area on the
ground level, parking spaces and a panoramic restaurant and garden

The study of a high-rise building on the
station square involves three sizes or scales;
the public space of the square, the quality
of the neighborhood, and the city skyline.
One understands the *a priori* interest in
constructing a landmark building in the
new station area, but is it necessary to do
so, and must one plonk it right on the
main square? This isn't a neighborhood
on the edges of the city, which stands
rejected. It's an interface between the
territory of the land (and the whole
country) and that of the city. The presence
of an architectural signifier, or a collection
of architectural signifiers consituting a
specific local skyline, gives the site an
identity, a particular character. Our task
consists in liberating the space of the
square in order to create a "real" station
square, the widest and largest possible.

Three scenarios have been studied:

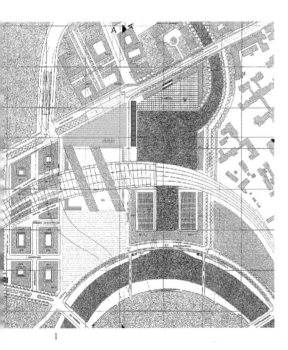

1

2

3

Scenario A – A tower beside the river Spree

If we pose the question of where best to build a tower in the central station area, our unequivocal reply is: beside the Spree, in front of the Tiergarten and the capital's government district. This site is worthy of the finest works of urban design, be they ancient, medieval or modern. The location is perfect for accommodating a "solitary", hence "unique", building. A tower, yes, but a tall, a very tall, tower. A building visible from all over Berlin, an unforgettable construction set in a prestigious landscape. Rarely has there been, in Berlin, such an obvious site for a skyscraper. As we see it, such an unusual, special case deserves to be put on the agenda.

1   Site plan for scheme C
2&3 Scheme C model of the skyscraper next to the Lehrter railway station

Scenario B – A tower on the far side of the square

The positioning of a tower on the square, as its background and parallel to the canal basin, goes with and qualifies the entrance to the station concourse by disengaging, freeing, and opening up the public space of the square to the surrounding town.

From the point of view of the buildings situated between the tower and the basin, however, the proximity of the tower is strong. To build along the street, on either side of it, is a truly urban ambition. We seek to ratify this urban type without being detrimental to the neighboring buildings. The idea of a huge lobby at the foot of the tower provides an architectural response to this urban situation. The height of the lobby is equal to that of the neighboring blocks of flats, namely around 25 to 27 meters. This lobby is faced entirely in clear glass. The tower emerges above the line of the roof, and ends at a height of 160 meters.

4

5

4   Front elevation, scheme C
5   Side elevation, scheme C
6   Model's side perspective, scheme C

6

Scenario C – A tower between the square and the canal basin

Pursuing the idea of opening up the space of the square to the maximum possible extent, we propose building not on the square itself but around it instead. To this end, and as an extension of the preceding idea, we have imagined emphasizing the station to the full with an urban square, and opening up this square onto the neighborhood and, in particular, onto the basin. Acting as a light filter, the tower – a glass sheet situated between earth and water – frames the square and allows for views towards the basin. The advantages of this position for a high-rise building are obvious: uninterrupted views and generous setbacks in relation to its neighbors. The building itself is larger, and is organized on the proportions of the triangle of the station square. It is not as tall as in the previous scenarios, the top of it reaching 144 meters.

7

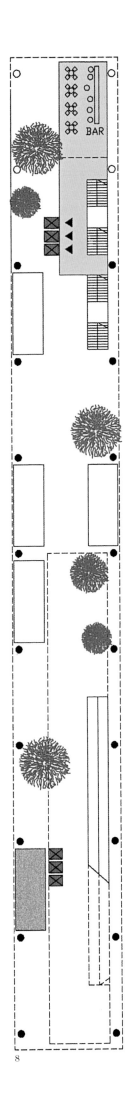

8

7   Aerial view of model, scheme C
8–12   Schematic plans of the most representative levels:
    8 Ground level
    9 Reception level
    10 Intermediate level over reception
    11 Typical office floor
    12 Terrace level

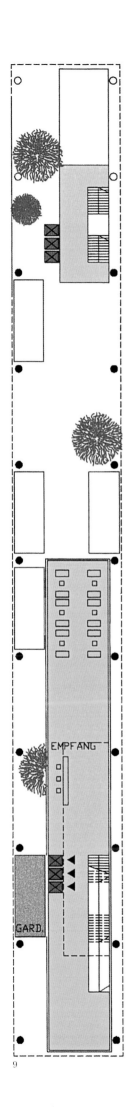

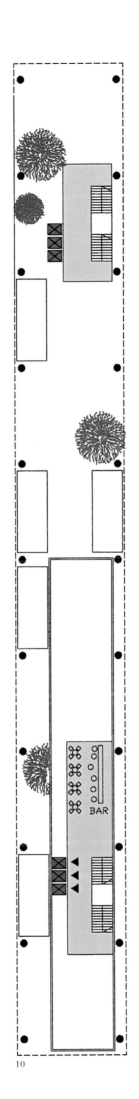

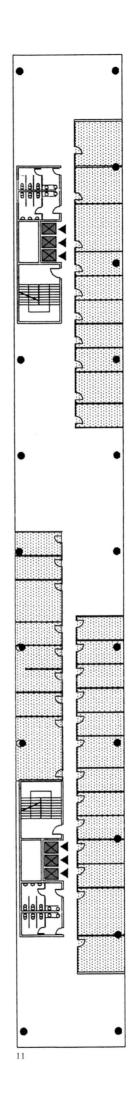

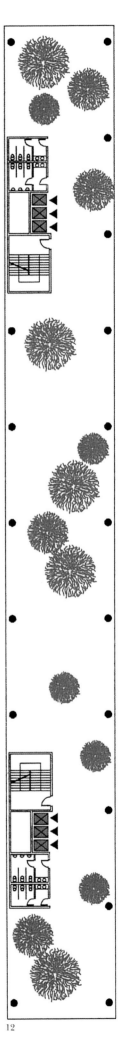

9

10

11

12

Central Media Library

Design/Completion 1997/2001, competition project–winner
Avenue Marcel Houël, Vénissieux, France
Client: City of Vénissieux
Surface: 4,000 m²
Cost: 38,500,000 FF (1998 value, before tax)
Program: Creation of reception hall, lecture reading rooms, offices, meeting halls, auditorium, and parking spaces

The Media Library is at garden height, flush with the meadow and its surroundings. This is a "large house" – a multi-purpose shelter, opening onto the town, opening onto the world. It's a place for learning about cultures, for a blending of sensibilities and a mixing of generations. We thought of building a glass box. Inside this, all the functions are brought together on the same level and girdled by a peristyle gallery.

This space encloses the different activities that take place in the Media Library and creates a "public" walkway between them. Taking a turn around the Media Library via the gallery is an enjoyable and instructive exercise. It is open onto the surroundings on one side, and onto the activities of the establishment on the other.

Continued

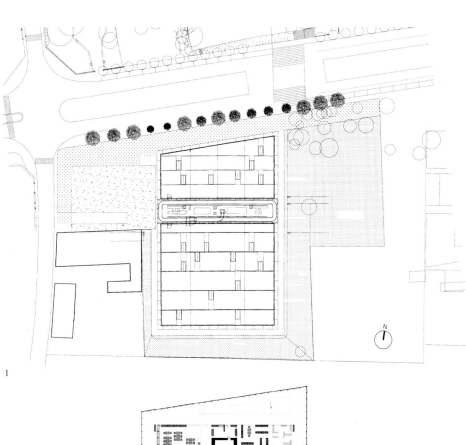

1

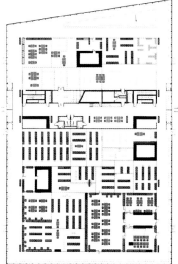

2

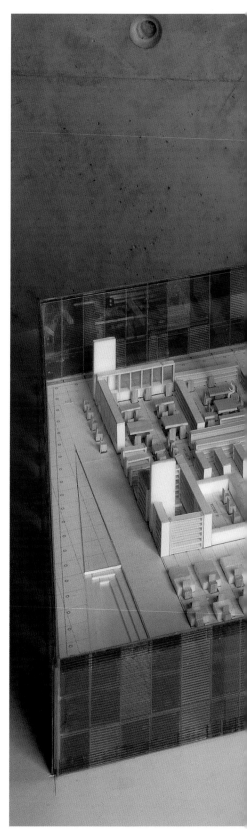

3

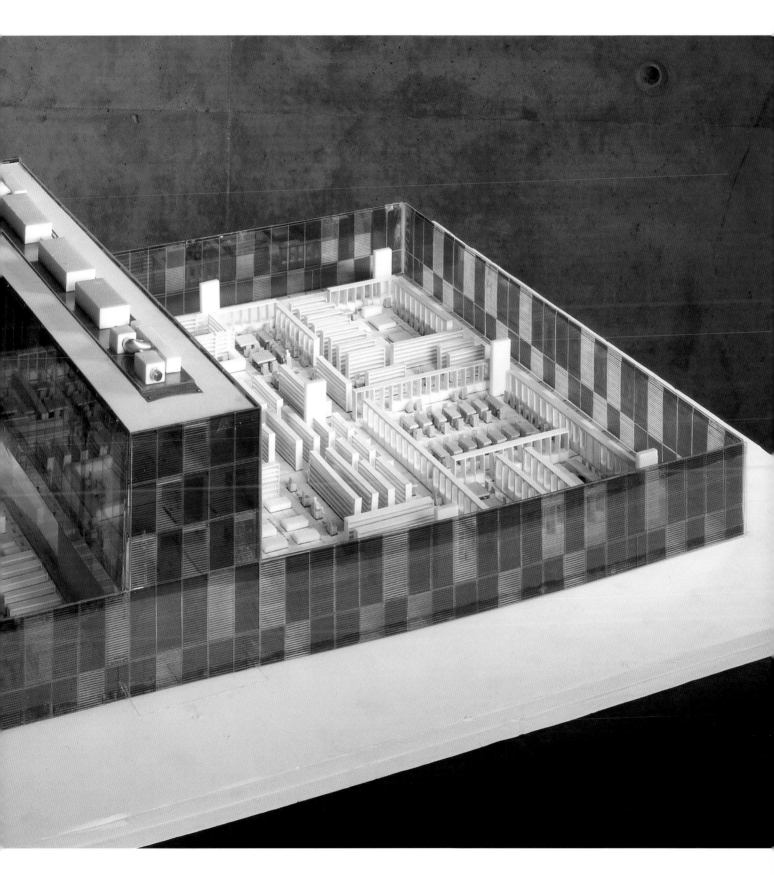

With no floors or hierarchy to speak of, the ease of getting around this large-house architecture makes it especially familiar.

At the heart of this assemblage, we find the entrance hall in the form of an urban passageway between the square (to the west) and the meadow (to the east). From this space we can get to the offices located in a small building placed on the roof of the large house.

This roof, this roofing, is pierced by different overhead openings, which bring daylight to the center of the building. The offices form an independent entity, yet are well connected to the activities of the Media Library, along the lines of those transparent objects that show us their workings. They expose the exchange operating between the facility and the citizen. The mobility and flexibility of the various spaces lends them a contemporary dimension linked to the movement of people and cultures.

Be they fixed, mobile, or fluttering like huge curtains, the partitioning elements are colored and made of a great variety of materials. We seek to create a gay and vibrant location in which "outside" and "inside" do not function by excluding each other, like some part or other of a wall. The economy of the scheme resides in its simplicity; the building is made up of a single ground floor for the Media Library and a small building for the services.

The entire construction is compact and treated with different "rough" materials: bare concrete, cement floors, galvanized steel structure, frosted and clear glass.

Energy saving results from the thickness of the building, which gives it excellent inertia and allows for thermal exchange between interdependent premises. This is also obtained through the double-skin enclosure produced by the gallery, which isolates the workings from the external atmosphere by acting as a thermal and sound buffer.

4   Master plan
5   Planning model
6   Perspective of access to the Media Library

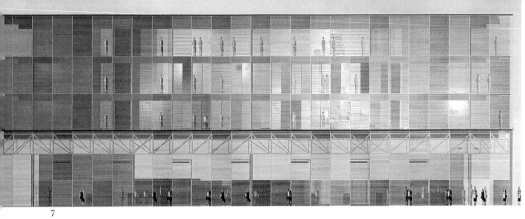

7

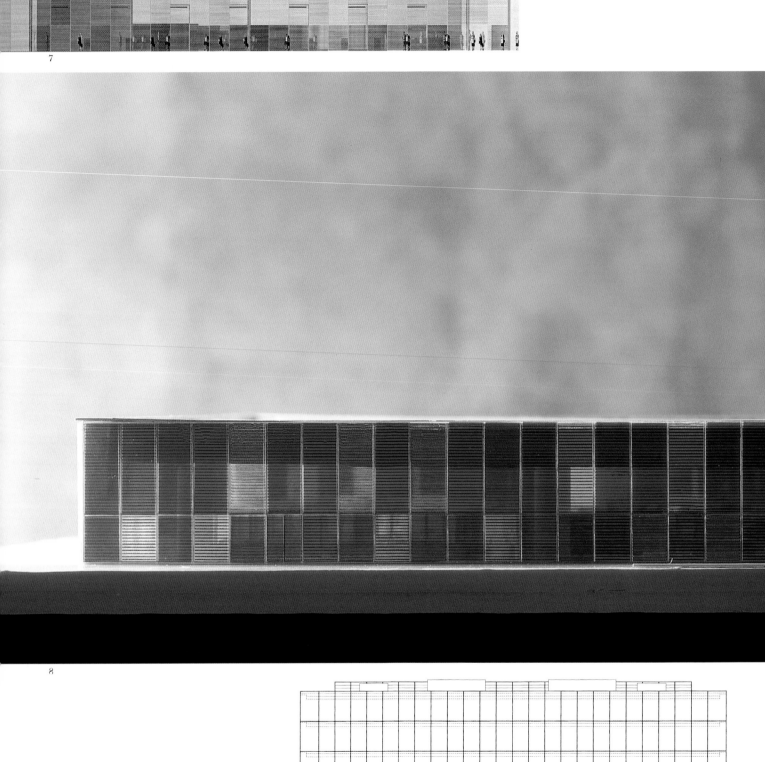

8

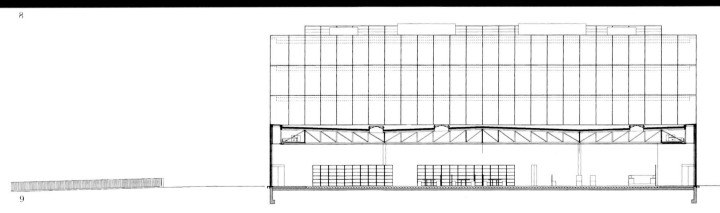

9

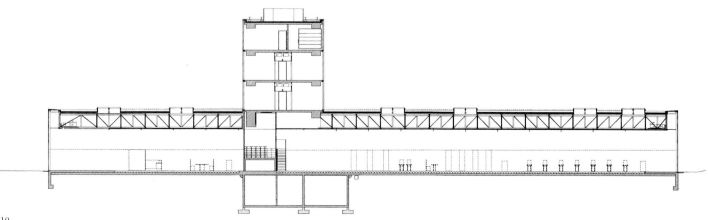

10

Hotels in the Antilles

Design/Studies 1998
Anse Tille (Gouadaloupe)/Cap Est (Martinique)/Montabo (Guyane)
Client: Groupe hotelier Fabre-Domergue
Surface: 17,000m² / 6,000m2/8.000m²
Program: Feasibility studies for four-star hotels and facilities

There were different sites on which the client wanted to create four-star hotels, including on the islands Gouadaloupe, Maritinique and Guyane. The three sites required three different approaches. One thing the hotels have in common is that each was the direct result of an understanding of the overwhelming landscape.

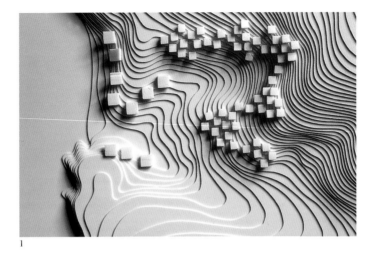

1

2

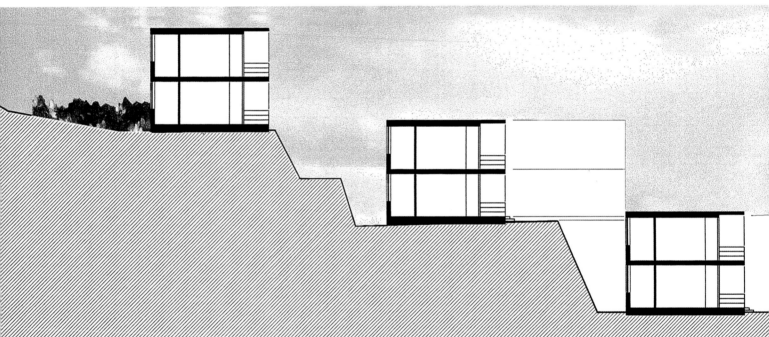

3

1   Model of the Anse Tille scheme (Guadaloupe)
2   Photograph of site, Anse Tille scheme
3   Cross section through accommodation pavilions,
    Anse Tille scheme
4   Plan, Anse Tille scheme

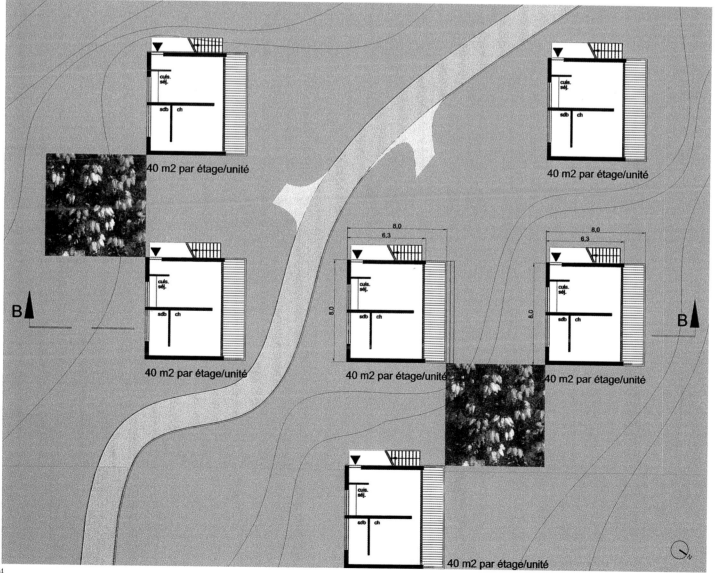

40 m2 par étage/unité

40 m2 par étage/unité

40 m2 par étage/unité

40 m2 par étage/unité

40 m2 par étage/unité

40 m2 par étage/unité

cuis.
séj.

sdb   ch

B

B

8,0

6,3

8,0

8,0

N

4

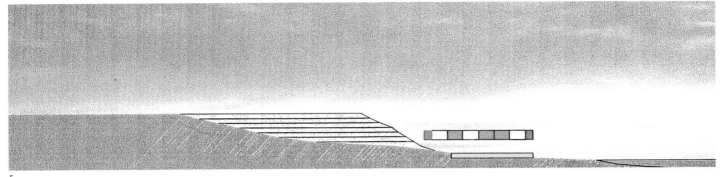

5

N

7

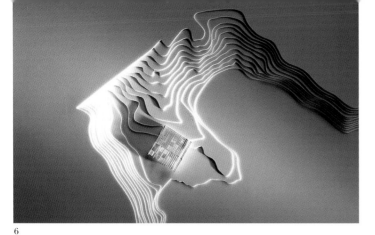

5 Section, Cap Est scheme (Martinique)
6 Model of the Cap Est scheme
7 Site plan for the Cap Est scheme
8 Typical schematic plan and section through
accommodations, Cap Est scheme

6

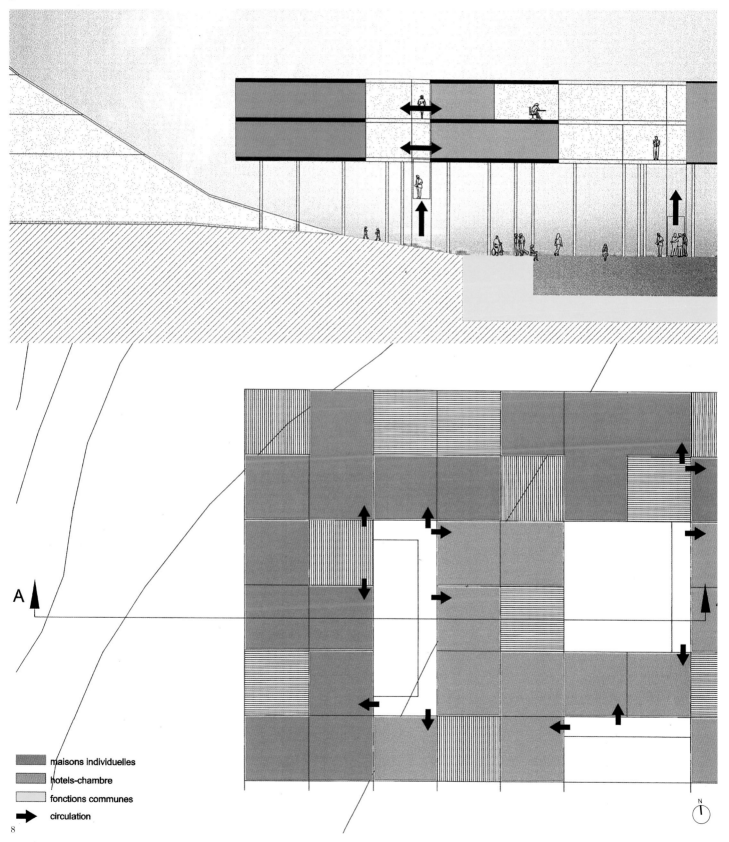

maisons individuelles
hotels-chambre
fonctions communes
circulation

8

9

10

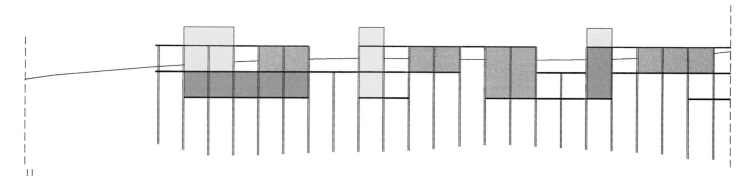

11

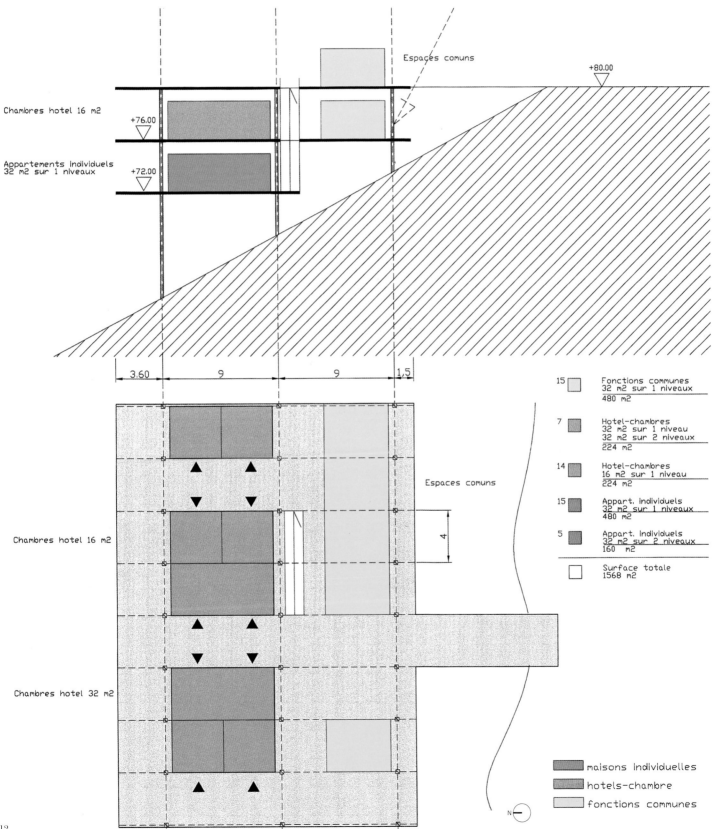

9   Model of the Montabo scheme (Guayane)
10 Photograph of site, Montabo scheme
11 Elevation from the sea, Montabo scheme
12 Typical schematic plan and section through
    accommodations, Montabo scheme

Espaces comuns

+80.00

Chambres hotel 16 m2   +76.00

Appartements individuels
32 m2 sur 1 niveaux   +72.00

3.60   9   9   1,5

15 Fonctions communes
    32 m2 sur 1 niveaux
    480 m2

7   Hotel-chambres
    32 m2 sur 1 niveau
    32 m2 sur 2 niveaux
    224 m2

14 Hotel-chambres
    16 m2 sur 1 niveau
    224 m2

15 Appart. individuels
    32 m2 sur 1 niveaux
    480 m2

5   Appart. individuels
    32 m2 sur 2 niveaux
    160 m2

    Surface totale
    1568 m2

Chambres hotel 16 m2

Espaces comuns

4

Chambres hotel 32 m2

maisons individuelles
hotels-chambre
fonctions communes

N

12

APLIX Factory

Design/Completion 1997/1999, winning architect after restricted
consultation
Zone d'Activités des Relandières, 44850 Le Cellier-sur-Loire,
Nantes Metropolitan Area, France
Client: APLIX S.A.
Surface: 30,000 m²
Cost: 65,000,000 FF (1997 value, before tax)
Architect's Mission: Complete engineering
Program: Self-gripping fastener production plant: plastic production
workshop, thermofixing, storage, offices, laboratories, social areas,
and landscaping

The factory is intended for the production
of "self-gripping systems" and synthetic-
fibre fabrics. Non-polluting for the
environment, this activity is of interest
to the community for the number of jobs
it will create following its opening. Its
potential for development will lend a
certain dynamism to the region. On top of
that, the design attempts to offer optimum
working conditions, and to guarantee a
flexible integration of future extensions.
This project, then, marks the beginning
of an industrial change in the community.

We have placed an orthogonal 20 ¥ 20 m
grid on top of the site, forming a
checkerboard of metal and vegetal
surfaces. The composition of the factory
itself is the result of the juxtaposition of
several 20 ¥ 20 m blocks, each 7.7 m high.
In the initial proposal, the form of the
factory is that of a long, regularly stepped
rectangle. The main facade gives onto the
main RN23 road; windowless, it expresses
the desire for interiorization linked to the
architectural project and to the
confidentiality of the activity of
production, with the strict design of a thin,
extended line from which a few treetops
protrude.

Continued

1

1   View of the factory from the national road
2   Study model, aerial view

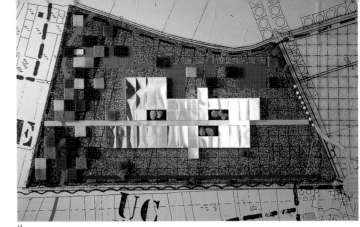

2

Running parallel to the RN23, the continuous and fluid space of an interior street, which constitutes the building's true backbone, allows for the circulation of forklift trucks and the intersection of the entire flow of raw materials and finished products. Three 20 X 40 m rectangular-based gardens, covered with lofty plantations, cling to the interior street; the russet bark and bluish foliage of pine trees, which will be 12 meters high by the end of construction work, provide them with a touch of color, while their airy tops allow the refracted light to enter the interior street. Around these gardens, and for each of the two divisions, the various workshops are organized according to the manufacturing cycle of the product.

Continued

3

3   Entrance façade
4   Detail
5   Aerial view under construction
6   Study model

4

5

6

The visible material is a slightly burnished metal sheeting. An idealized expression of agricultural buildings, it reflects the surrounding nature and allows the factory to gently blend into it. Each part of the project is conceived so as to enable the envisaging of workshop extensions and parking areas. For this reason, the rigorous conception of the composition's masses and their effects remains subject to variation. Extensions are possible via the aleatory articulation of supplementary squares, which would thus create visual irregularities, notably in the frontal view. For the moment, then, there is no definitive configuration of the extensions to the factory, but rather the wish for a game of chance elicited by the metal/vegetal encounter of volumes and reflections.

7

8

7   Factory entrance
8   Truck delivery area

9

10

11

The Museum of Modern Art

Design Competition 1997, competition project
West 53rd Street, New York, New York, U.S.A.
Client: Museum of Modern Art
Surface: 47,660 m²
Program: Galleries for permanent and temporary exhibitions, conference halls, offices, stock spaces, conservation spaces, restaurants for employees, public cafeteria, library, and bookshop

The work presented here constitutes an open-ended architectural investigation. It is not a catalogue of projects; instead, proceeding from an analysis of context, we have established a diagnosis that presents different potential responses. The interest this diagnosis has resides, on the one hand, in the identification of elements to be protected, and on the other, in that of the elements to be designed and projected. The first form the system's common trunk; the rest constitute the Museum's developments and metamorphoses.

Urban analysis shows the difference in nature and function between 53rd and 54th Streets; one is more pedestrian-oriented. This opposition constitutes a specific urban feature of the MoMA: it has a street (53rd) side and a garden (54th) side. This reading of the site clarifies the urban situation by dividing, lengthwise, the block: built on 53rd Street, open towards 54th. It cannot, though, be said that there is a "front" and a "back", but rather a streetside Museum and a gardenside Museum.

The organizational structure of the MoMA can be compared to a tree. It digs down into the earth as if searching for its "life force" there. In an opposed movement, it thrusts a long built mass emphatically upwards to form its "trunk". Then, blossoming out, it extends its branching structure – its "treetop" – aside, above

Continued

1

PRESENCE OF MOMA in NYC

TOWER

MUSEUM OF MODERN ART

GARDEN

identity bloc

2

1   Model of the "Above" scheme
2   Sketch
3   Interior perspective
4   Concept sketches of the three schemes

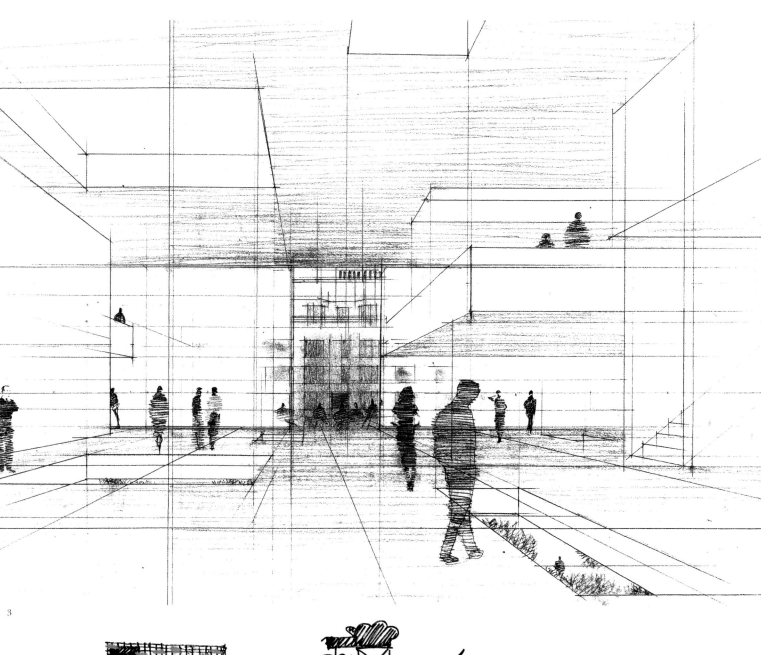

3

above

aside

along

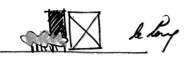

4

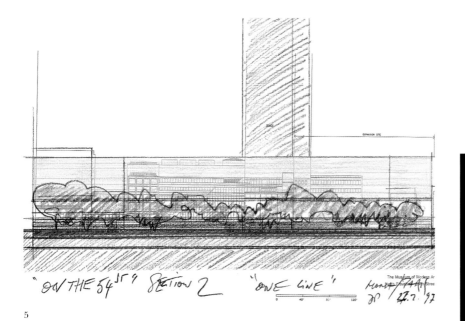

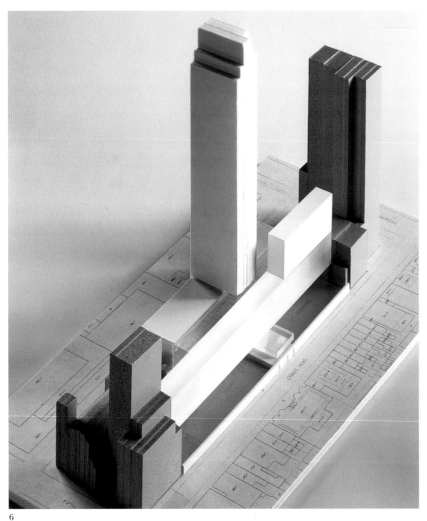

5   Section drawing of the "Along" scheme
6   Concept model of the "Along" scheme
7   Model of the "Along" scheme, view from 54th street

and along. Crowning the whole thing, the tower soars up into the sky, where it participates in the aerial concert of its no less prestigious neighbors.

Since we are evoking roots and branches, it is fitting, first, to elaborate a trunk. This element forms the core of the project. Architectural and functional analysis of the existing building shows that the exhibition rooms do not have their place, or more precisely their "correct place", there. By freeing the floors currently given over to exhibitions, and by moving the library and conservation departments there, we put the existing building to better use as regards its organization and the quality of its work spaces. The enlarged and more ventilated offices occupy the upper part of the building and all benefit from natural light.

Forming part of the same undertaking, the extension of the garden hall to the whole of the building (both length- and height-wise) creates a place full of life and movement, bathed in natural light, with all levels being served by a set of vertical and horizontal circulations.

By following, developing, and amplifying the morphology of the existing building, the trunk, the life-giving element of the MoMA, is thus formed.

Starting from the trunk, three potential positions for the Museum's exhibition rooms could be imagined: aside, along and above it. The last option was the most accurate and contemporary.

Continued

8

8   Model of the "Aside" scheme, view from 54th street
9   Section drawing of the "Along" scheme
10   Concept model for the "Aside" scheme

9

0

Above

In pursuing the investigation of an architectural expansion for the exhibition galleries from a single common trunk, the possibility emerged of building above:

- a roof for human occupation, floating above the garden and covering the existing building;

- a roof, like a huge, thin leaf, unifying the diversity of the buildings – a shelter in the mythical sense of the original house, which protects the human group and its culture from the hostility of the world;

Continued

The Museum of Modern Art   101

- a roof bathed in light and air, permeable to light and water, allowing each to pass at certain places and permitting the garden to "breathe" according to its natural rhythm;

- a roof between sky and earth, bordering 54th Street, without walling it off or shading it;

- a roof crowning the 53rd Street buildings, defined as artists' studios that would form an extended glass attic;

- a roof whose length offers a wide range of planning possibilities, and a flexibility in relation to the administration and growth of the collections;

- a roof in which the Museum tour is flexible and free;

- a roof that gives the MoMA its identity as a cultural building, yet one that is largely open to the public;

- a roof in keeping with the sensibility and vision of contemporary art, like an "installation" that gives an "other" meaning to the site as a whole – a metamorphosis, or transfiguration even, of the place itself;

- a roof lending identity to the site, while preserving the difference between its parts, like some reference to the notion of democracy described by Monsieur de Tocqueville;

- a roof that causes us to fantasize about an architecture freed from gravitational pull – a certain idea of immateriality.

12

TOWER

EL. 174'-0"

MECH.   EL. 147'-

6TH FL.   EL. 136'-

5TH FL.   EL. 124'-8"

4TH FL.   EL. 110'-5"

3RD FL.   EL. 96'-2"

2ND FL.   EL. 81'-6"

GROUND FL.   EL. 67'-4"

GARDEN

TITUS I THEATER

SUBCELLAR   EL. 42'-6"

13

11   Study model of the "Above" scheme
12   Concept model for the "Above" scheme
13   Section drawing of the "Above" scheme

Kansai-Kan Library

Design Competition 1996, competition project
Kansai-Kan, Seika-cho, Kyoto, Japan
Client: National Diet Library, Japanese Ministry of Construction
Surface: 56,000 m²
Program: stockrooms (26,000 m²), research reading rooms (6,000 m²),
administration (4,000 m²), conference rooms (3,000 m²),
diverse rooms (12,000 m²), and technical rooms (5,000 m²)

Three gardens for the library

The Natural Garden

Once upon a time there was Nature, before we (humankind) cleared it and established our towns there. Today we are in search of that part of ourselves we once believed we could do without. A bit of nature as a place to live – what could be more "natural" for a large library?

A vast wooden esplanade forms a wide drive; it is bordered by pines planted on a carpet of moss and well mown grass. The trees, whose contours are to be shaped over the years, will create a foliate skyline fixed at the same height as the projecting glass of the library.

The Glass Garden

All but nothing, just a flash of light, a scintillating line; such is the immaterial and poetic sign of the Library's presence.

A sheet of glass with its changing reflections that irresistibly attract the eye. You make your way towards this "crystal" and enter a garden of glass. As in a huge kaleidoscope or telescope lens, the views are multiplied and intersect to infinity, blending the surrounding nature with the serene world of the reading rooms. This filter protects the Library, tactfully covers it. This is the entrance, the reception area, the meeting place, the interface between inside and out.

The Reading Garden

At the heart of the Library a huge space bathed in gentle, diffused overhead light accommodates and subsumes the various functions related to reading. As if in a garden, you discover small box-like constructions wrapped in fabric. Absorbing the sound, these "objects" delimit the calm, human-sized reading areas. The light in this world is indirect and all movement silent.

Continued

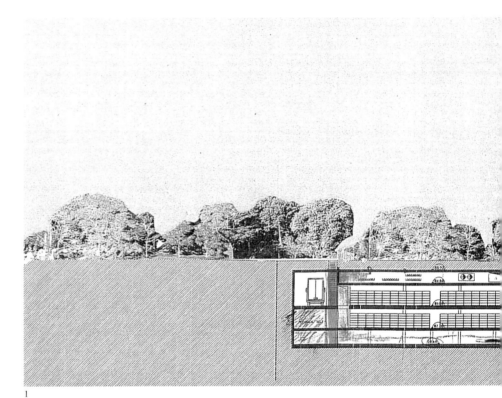

1

1 Cross section of the library
2 Overall view of the site
3 Main entrance to the Library via the roof

2

104

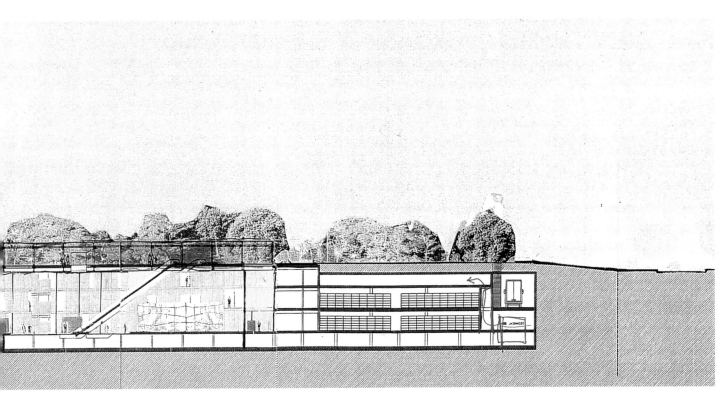

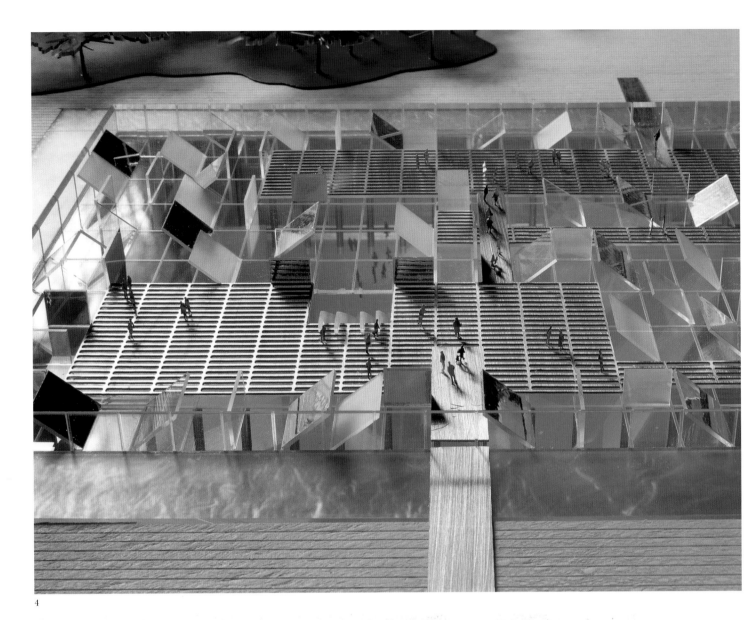

4

5

Four Organizational Plans

The Readers

The readers are at the center of the Library, at the heart of the book-issuing system and right beside the librarians. In this huge room, the arrangement is flexible to suit the needs of the readers, the scientific evolution of the collections, and any technological transformations in ways of reading.

The Personnel

The librarians and their services surround the reading areas. This ring, or belt, constitutes the interface between the large reading room (communication) and the book stacks (conservation).

The Books

The books are distributed around the edges of the reading rooms; since there is no natural light, they are protected from the "outside world". The organization of the stacks is highly compact, in order to reduce the distance and time of transport.

The Future Extension

The extension follows the form of the ground. The natural garden is prolonged as far as the hill, and the basement book storage areas follow the unfolding of the landscape. The extension can be undertaken in several stages. Its organisation is the geometrical continuation of the first phase.

4   View of the filter roof that covers and protects the library reading rooms
5   Longitudinal section through reading rooms, storage, and service areas
6   View of the glass reflecting cover at night

6

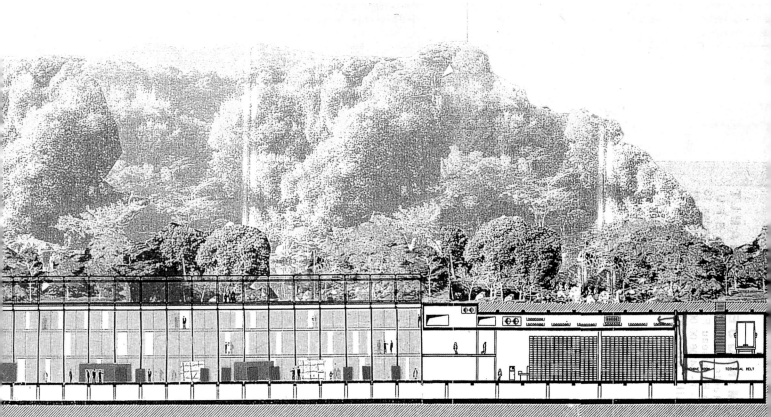

Great Extension of the European Union Court of Justice

Design/Completion 1996/2007
Luxemburg, Luxemburg
Client: Administration of Public Buildings and the European Union Court of Justice
Architect Partnership: Bohdan Paczowski & Paul Fritsch, M3
Surface: 96,000 m²
Program: Fourth extension of the Court of Justice of the European Union; creation of 24,000 m² of offices, of which 12,000 m² are for the judges; 20,000 m² of public facilities with conference rooms, libraries, and restaurant; asbestos removal and renovation of the existing law courts (25,000 m²) and services

The Law Court building was initiated at the beginning of the 1960s, following an architectural competition won by the Conzemius Group from Luxemburg and Jamage & Van der Elste from Liege. Following occupation of the premises in 1973, it was realized that this building was already too small, and that it was necessary to consider future extensions to it. The Milan architect Bohdan Paczowski, creator of the design for the Jean Monnet building next door to the Law Court building, was commissioned at the end of 1978 to work on the extension project, in association with the Luxemburg architects Fritsch, Herr, Huyberechts and Van Driessche. This entailed an extension of some 80,000 square meters, to be realized during three phases of construction. The extension was not to work in opposition to the existing building, but its parameters were to be extrapolated so as to form a coherent continuation of it.

Continued

1

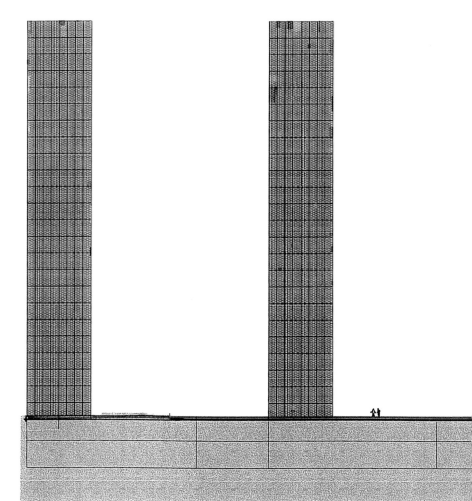

1 Overall view of the site: presentation model of the existing Court of Justice and the new extension buildings
2 Longitudinal section
3 Ground level

2

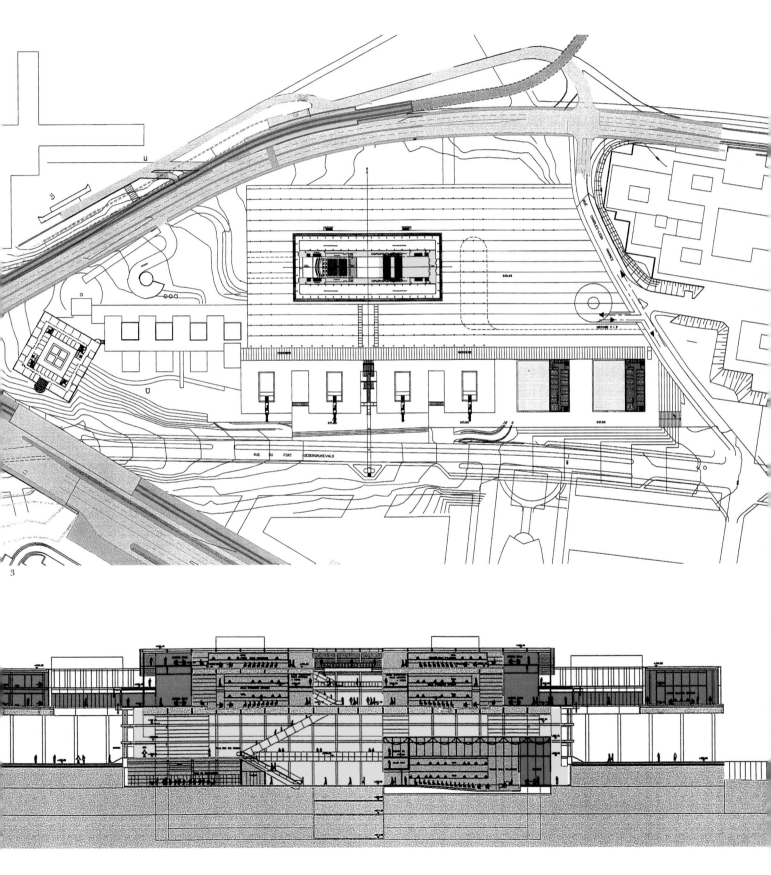

3

The Law Court building, placed on a
raised plinth and endowed with imposing
cantilevers and colonnade, is set out
according to a rigorous symmetry. Account
being taken of its central and isolated
position, it was impossible to imagine an
extension simply continuing the existing
building. It was necessary to seek a
solution that respected the identity of the
building, but also responded to a concern
for perfect osmosis of the whole. The
architects therefore chose an architectural
approach that exploited the site's
extremely steep slope. The greater part of
the new building is inscribed in the lower
slope of the Law Court building, and
leaves the view of the latter completely
unobstructed. The first construction phase
follows the symmetry of the original
building, somehow reinforcing the plinth
image. The second phase, a wave form,
goes to form the ramparts. The third,
more compact, phase represents a castle
with four towers. This building, at a
distance from the existing one, is the only
one higher than the plinth. The whole
project is deliberately conceived according
to a typology close to the idea of a
defensive wall, a fortress like the city of
Luxemburg itself. The pink Breton granite
coherently relates to the rust-colored
Continued

4

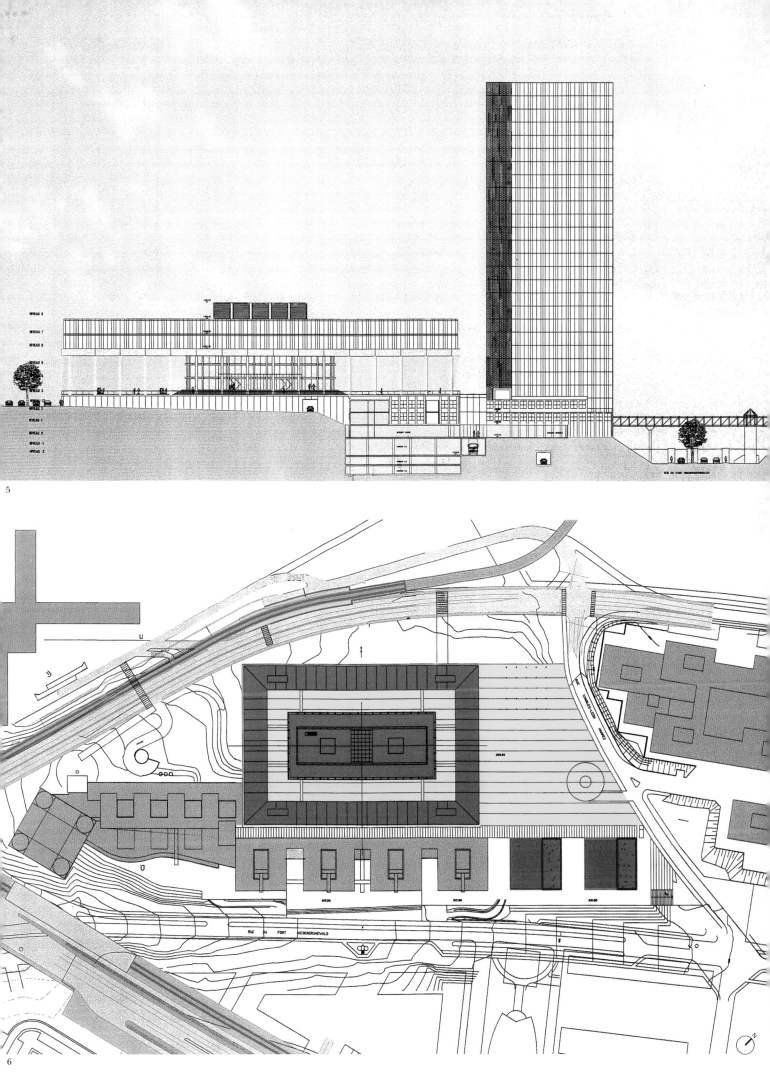

5

6

original building. Once these extensions were completed in 1994, the question of further extensions was raised once more. On top of that, the original building, riddled with asbestos, had to be cleaned up and reorganized.

In 1994 a town planning competition awarded a Luxemburg team, made up of the architectural studios Paczowski & Fritsch and Flammang & Lister, the commission for the new Law Court building and its large-scale extension. Following an approach from them, Dominique Perrault accepted an offer to be part of the new team for this commission, with the agreement of the Luxemburg Government. Dominique Perrault is the author of this new project, presented to the European Court in December 1998.

Paul Fritsch and Bohdan Paczowski

Architect Paul Fritsch has worked in Luxemburg since 1971, when he created his office. Architect Bohdan Paczowski graduated in Cracow and Milan. He worked mainly in Italy until 1983. They have been partners since 1989, when they created their architectural office in Luxemburg.

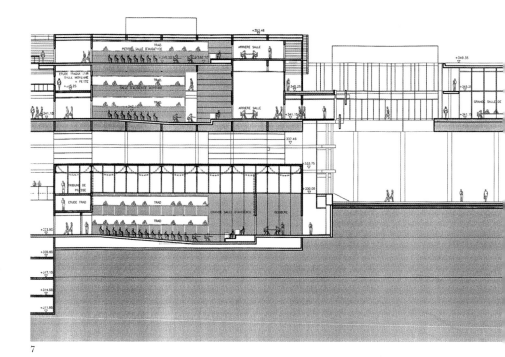

7

7   Section through the axis of the existing Court of Justice and new extension: audience rooms
8&9   Entrance esplanade

8

112

9

Kolonihavehus Installation

Design/Completion 1996/1996
Copenhagen, Denmark
Client: Fondation Kolonihavehus and City of Copenhagen
Surface: 5 m²
Mission: Design and execution drawings
Program: Conception of a "Kolonihaven"-type installation for an exposition held in Copenhagen in 1996, when that city was the cultural capital of Europe

"A house, a tree" and an enclosure: this is the Kolonihaven typology. Nature "of one's own", a bit of ground "of one's own" and a house that expresses the inhabitant's sensibility. Expressive, gay, exotic... but above all unique. This tiny territory with its tree is a treasure. It opens onto the environment in order to assert itself and thereby "live together" with it. An enclosure of four sheets of glass stakes its claim. This glass box harnesses nature, which is then possessed and shared by man.

The real nature of our nature; what other nature is there?

1

2

1   View of the installation in the park: computer simulation
2   Detail of the glass enclosure
3&4   Nature harnessed by the glass box during the winter

3

4

Innsbruck Town Hall

Design/Completion 1998/2002, competition project–winner
Adolf-Pichler-Platz, Fallmerayerstrasse, Innsbruck, Austria
Client: Town of Innsbruck, Projektgesellschaft Town Hall Innsbruck
Associated Architect: Rolf Reichert, R.P.M. Munich
Surface: 40,000 m²
Cost: 400,000,000 FF (1998 value, before tax)
Architect's Mission: Renovation and extension of the Town Hall of
Innsbruck, covering of a public passage·
Program: offices, meeting rooms, restaurant, private garden on the roof,
commercial gallery, parking spaces, and four-star hotel

When, in the spring of 1996, the town of Innsbruck invited him to participate in an international competition for the Town Hall Passage, Dominique Perrault suggested we collaborate with him in the realization of the project. Thanks to the confidence gained as a consequence of our extended participation in the Berlin Olympic cycle track and swimming pool project, and due to his experience of the thought processes and work methods of the Germans – acquired on the Salzburg and Munich competitions, among others –

he was sure, right from the start, that for this difficult project in the town center it was vital to have a collaborator who spoke German.

In a project as complex and important for the town of Innsbruck as this one, not only do the urbanistic and formal aspects play an important role, but the political ones do too. For that reason, an exact understanding of the parameters within which a project like this one may become possible is essential. Along with a knowledge of the German language, it is

essential to sense, understand, and correctly apply both the way of thinking of the sponsors of the competition, and the political environment. Not having taken these factors into account is, among others, the reason why most entries, especially the foreign ones – with the exception of Guido Canali's – were completely mistaken, in my opinion and also in the opinion of the jury.

During the preparatory phase of the competition, which took place

Continued

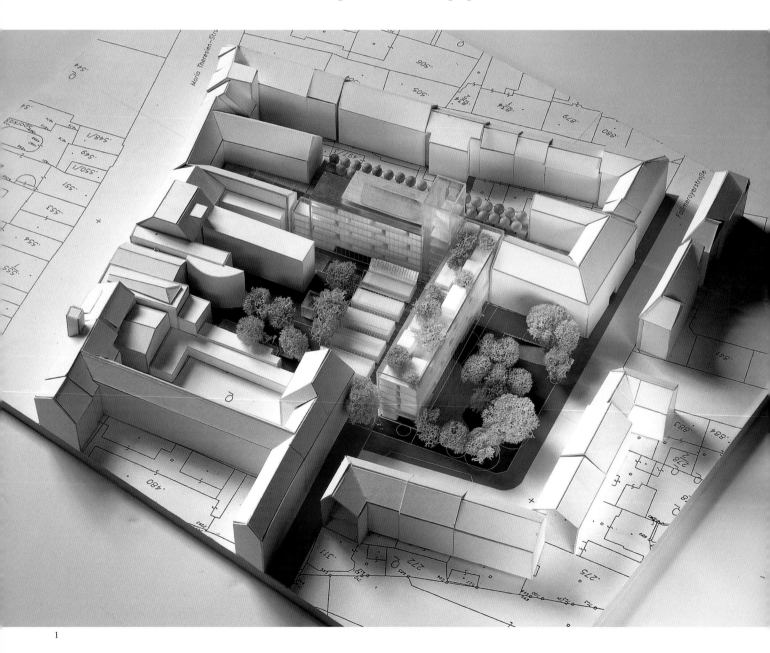

1

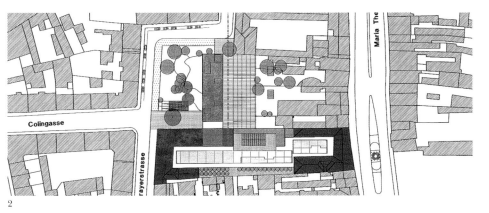

1 Overall site view of study model
2 Site plan
3 Study model of the hotel, the town hall, and the
commercial gallery

4

concurrently in Paris and Munich – first by
fax, then by e-mail – the sketches
originating in Paris were continually being
screened and adapted to what was feasible
and justifiable within the framework of the
complex pre-existing factors. Dominique
meant for the design to be not only
spectacular, as the Munich one had been,
but also for it to respect, echo and
complement the characteristics of the site.
For our part, we were hoping to endow
this area of the town with a new urban
entity that was recognizable and up-to-
date, although modest in size. We
therefore proposed a Town Hall with a
tower and balcony, with which the town
could easily identify itself.

Unfortunately, the private investors
considered that the part corresponding to
the retail area did not adequately fulfil
their expectations, and so the jury called
for a second phase of the competition,
restricted to our team and that of Guido
Canali. Regrettably, a restructuring of the
private investment involved paralysed all
deliberation for a year and a half.

In January 1998, the jury met again and
decided, unanimously this time, to select
our project alone for future development.
According to the jury, it was the one that
responded most satisfactorily to the
urbanistic, formal and functional demands
of the program, within the confines of
which the requirements of commercial
exploitation were also adequately fulfilled.

Rolf Reichert

Rolf Reichert, Architect, is a partner at
Atelier Reichert–Pranschke–Maluche
Architekten (R.P.M.), Munich. He is a
member of the Urban Planning
Commission of Munich and Co-Director of
the Institute of Architects of Bavaria. Since
1993, he has been an associate of
Dominique Perrault for the construction
of the Olympic velodrome and swimming
pool in Berlin.

5

Pre-landscaping and Redevelopment of the UNIMETAL Site

Design/Completion 1995/1997, competition project–winner
Orne River Banks, Normandie, France
Client: District du Grand Caen

Architect's Mission: Consultant architect for the District of Grand Caen, creation of a guide plan in the north-east of the District (transport plans), redevelopment of disused industrial areas following the disappearance of the iron and steel industry (250 ha)

Architect's Activities: Creation of a database (studies, meetings); analysis of the town planning (history and geography); urban development scheme: creation of sections on the Orne River Banks, creation of the urban development control and zoning plan (north-east of the agglomeration)

The issue here was not so much historical as geographical. The disappearance of an asset like the Société Métallurgique de Normandie (SMN) can also create new opportunities which would help bring nature to the town.

To identify the assets and potentialities of the site and, proceeding from these, to define what the future might hold. Here, no vast layouts, no "new town," but the savage desire to connect and reconnect nature and architecture.

To detect three significant locations: the valley site, the plateau, the ridge. Along the River Orne, a wide avenue planted with beautiful trees asks for nothing more than being bordered by the continuum of buildings that defines a town. On the plateau, traces of the former SMN facilities guide and prefigure the lines interweaving countryside and urbanization. At the head of the valley, the layout of an old road that crossed the factory demands only to be linked to the neighboring areas of the town. To attempt, then, to draw what is most essential from each location. To devise a wide-ranging project that will blend the different activities and, above all, be able to introduce other types of relationship with nature. The project attempts to qualify the locations by giving them an identity, a future.

The relationship between the plateau and the valley deserves protection, respect and enhancement. The problem is not an absence, but an excess, of ground. The redefinition of the town extends to the riverbanks and the hillsides and, from there, to the entire site.

1

2

3 Tree plantations and remediation of the
  polluted site
4 Installation of evening lighting on the existing
  landmark (the old aerorefigerator)
5 Distribution of activities
6 Aerial view of the pre-landscaping project with
  existing landmarks
7&8 Tree plantations and polluted earth
  remediation

3

4

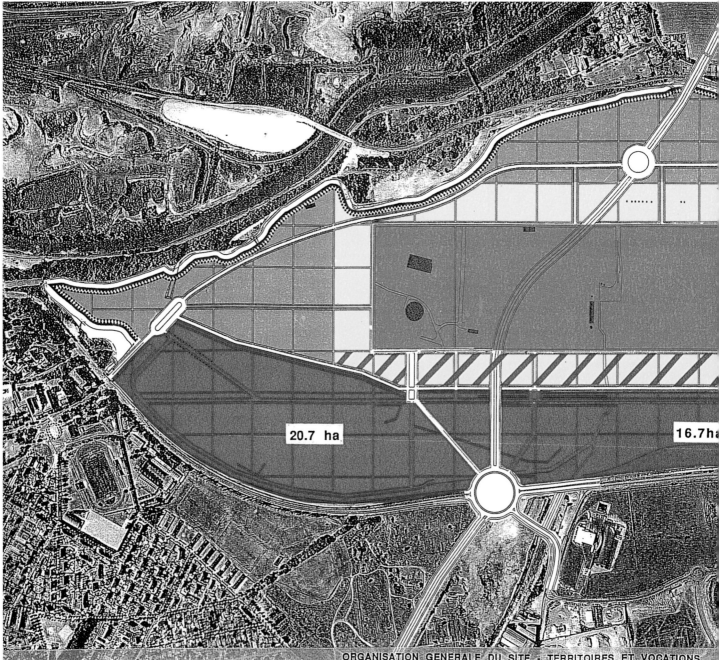

20.7 ha

16.7 ha

ORGANISATION GENERALE DU SITE - TERRITOIRES ET VOCATIONS

5

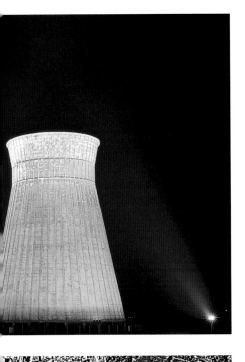

6

7

8

Headquarters of Bayerische Hypotheken und Wechselbank

Design Competition 1994, competition project
Theatinerstrasse, Munich, Germany
Client: Bayerische Hypotheken-und-Wechselbank
Surface: 97,000 m²
Program: Offices, art gallery, commerce, services, restaurants, and housing

Our proposal was aimed at combining the historical organization of the city and the construction of a present-day building. We consequently retained the "outer shell" of the block so as to not tamper with the character of the historic centre. The architecture of these roadside buildings may be considered somewhat ordinary, but they do have the immense quality of "being there". We go along with what exists, not against it.

When a modern building is introduced or even, as it were, "inlaid" in the middle of a block, it may well become lost. In other words, it may well appear "recessed" in relation to the thoroughfares and structures of the neighbourhood.

What is at issue, though, is the creation of an organic entity in which and through which a network of movement, linkage, and circulation is woven together. This said, there is also the matter of the endeavour to show up the charms of the old town, and in particular its architecture, its colours, and its symbols, by creating a large panoramic viewpoint, like a large roof garden, from which one can survey Munich.

The project might in fact be described as a "slice" of the city, in which people move about with ease and fluidity from ancient to modern, and bottom to top, with the greatest of freedom.

The admixture of history and function forms a unique landscape that provides a sign of today – a complementary identity for the fragile and vulnerable district that is Munich's city centre.

The project can be seen as the blending of an architectural concept and an urban context. It is not cut and dried, for our aims are clear, but flexible, too. It is a fact that the right compatibility between a building and the city should be the fruit of patient, painstaking work involving one and all. And everyone bears the weight of responsibility for it.

We offer a method of open-minded design that is intended to lead to a consensus between high architectural quality and a far-reaching concern for the evolution of our contemporary society.

1

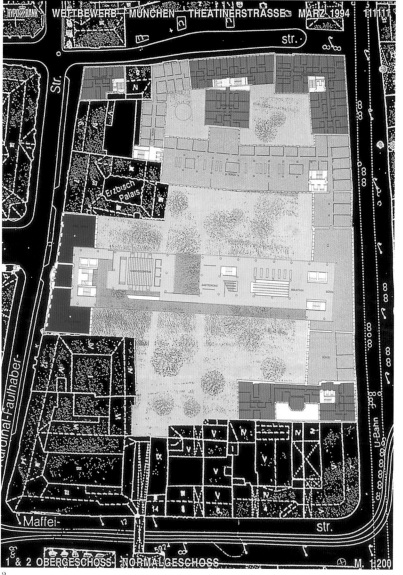

2

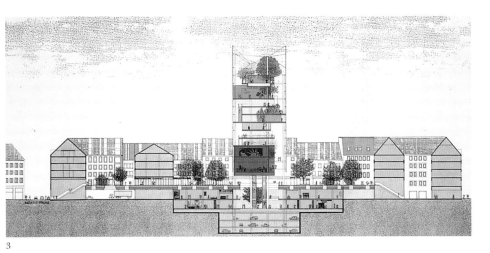

1 Presentation model
2 Site plan
3 Cross section
4 Perspective

3

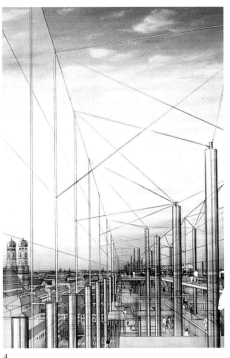

4

Private Villa

Design/Completion 1992/1995
Bretagne, France
Private client
Engineer: Guy Morisseau
Constructed surface 400 m², garden 4,000 m²
Program: Villa for a family containing six bedrooms (with bathroom),
a kitchen, two dressing rooms, a large living-room and a play area

This house, is it really a house? That's the question, or self-questioning, we deliberately set ourselves.

Architecture's presence or absence is a persistent theme of reflection in our work, which is increasingly concerned with the question of LANDSCAPE as a linking element between ARCHITECTURE and NATURE.

Can one live underground? Can one rediscover the cave of humanity's earliest times as the subjective foundation of our presence on the Earth? This architecture is an experiment, a ceaselessly renewed experiment aimed at understanding, feeling, trying to live better with/in our surroundings. Such research into sentient emotions, which can be understood only by physically living them, makes one think of the idea developed by the painter Francis Bacon with regard to emotion in painting, which ought to reach the brain without passing through the intellect.
Genius loci, the INDIVIDUAL'S happiness: two good reasons for us, as architects, to build things, thereby showing that conventional commonplaces and preconceptions are not the only rules of ART – to which the conformism of our contemporary societies too often refers itself.

1

2

3

4

5

1&2   View of the façade from the garden
3–5   The house in relation to its natural surroundings, protecting sunshade, and glass façade

The Grand Stadium

Design Competition 1993, winning project
New town of Melun-Senart, outskirts of Paris, France
Client: Government of France and New Town of Melun-Senart
Team: Dominique Perrault [planning and project manager, Pierre Ferret (architect specialist in stadiums)] and HOK (covering structure)
Engineering Consultants: Fougerolle, SPIE, SAE
Project, landscape and town planning on an area of 100 ha
Cost: 3,000,000,000 FF (1993 value, after tax)
Program: Stadium for the football world championship in 1998 – 85,000 seats, 12,000 parking spaces and training stadium; landscape and town planning for the environment of the stadium

The center of the new town of Melun-Senart is criss-crossed by a dense complex of motorway and rail systems, with their interchanges and switches. Their impact is extremely constraining to the harmonious development of an urban fabric, but also highly necessary for a town endowed with life.

Based on a reading of the town's forms and layouts, we can conclude that the stadium's context is of primary importance in defining the entrance to the town center, and acts as a sign or reference point as the town is crossed along the motorway. Nevertheless, its strong presence and the functions it houses should not disturb the life of the town, but work alongside it. The presence and absence of the stadium is the urban issue at stake – a "squaring of the circle" that must be resolved. The presence of a major sporting facility, on both a national and international scale, brings media attention to Melun-Senart, and thus a bit of life and

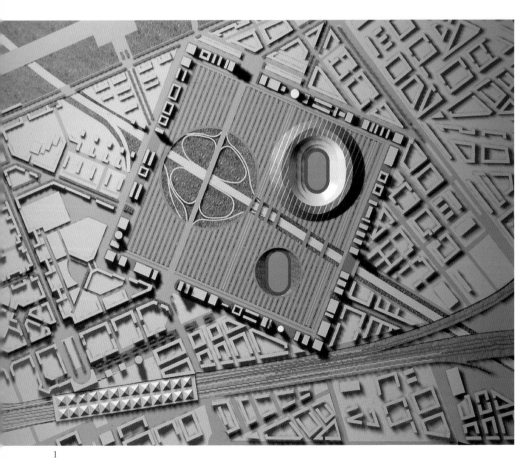

1

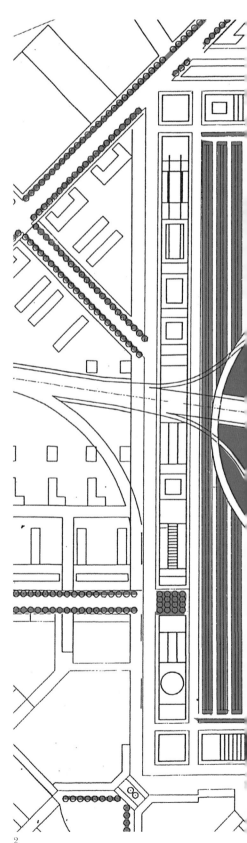

2

128

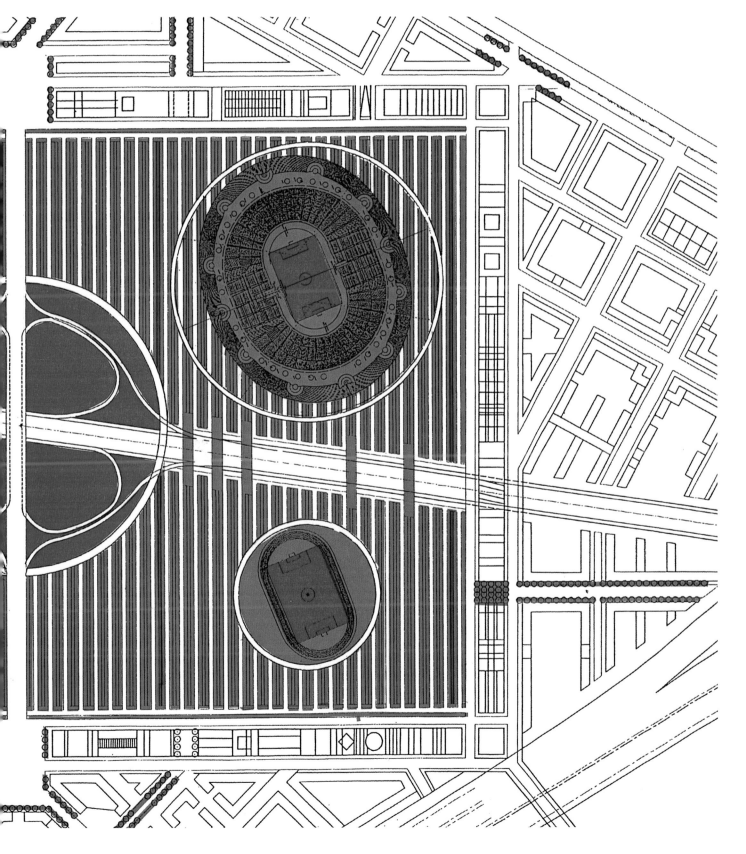

recognition for the town *vis-à-vis* the planning of the region. Absence of the same wished-for sporting facility when it is empty and when it neutralizes, with its immense retinue of parking lots, a vast central area of the town produces a wish to conceal it.

The urban part seeks to integrate, in one and the same stretch of landscape, four giant facilities: a motorway interchange, a vast stadium, the training stadium, and thousands of parking places. Proceeding from the idea of landscape handled in a contemporary way, without ecological complacency, but with a respect for all that is precious in the town center – namely, empty space – we have constructed a symbolic form that groups the town around a natural site. The idea of landscape in the wider sense, of the rediscovery of Nature and Town, seemed to us to be the locus and the link that would combine to create an identity proper to Melun-Senart.

3

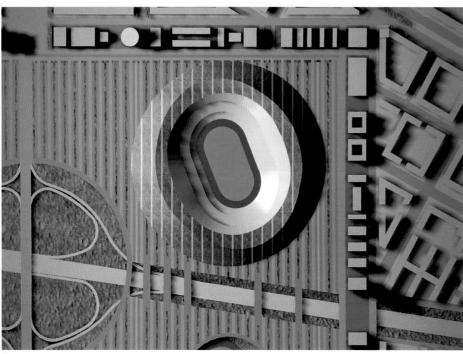

4

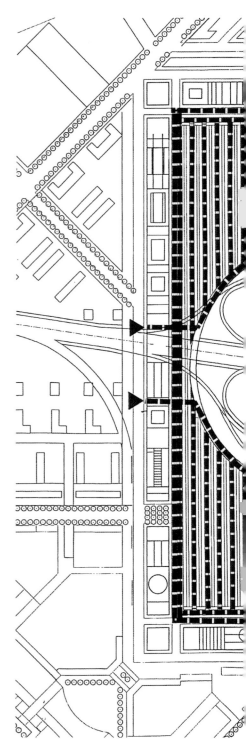

5

3   Computer aerial view
4   Main stadium
5   Site plan networks

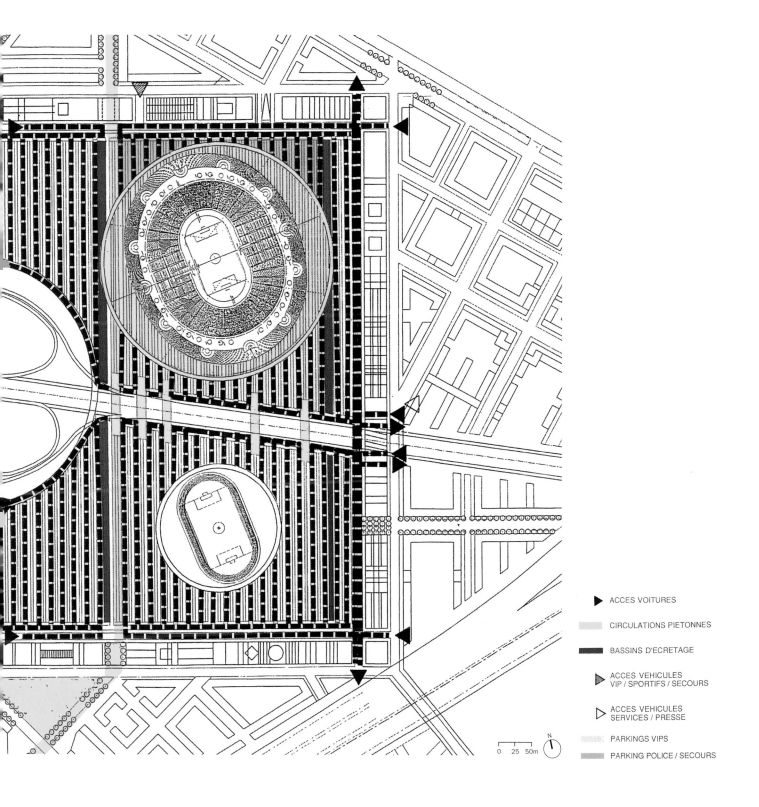

ACCES VOITURES

CIRCULATIONS PIETONNES

BASSINS D'ECRETAGE

ACCES VEHICULES
VIP / SPORTIFS / SECOURS

ACCES VEHICULES
SERVICES / PRESSE

PARKINGS VIPS

PARKING POLICE / SECOURS

0 25 50m   N

The Great Greenhouse,
Cité des Sciences et de l'Industrie

Design/Completion 1995/1997, competition project–winner
Cité des Sciences et de l'Industrie, Paris, France
Client: Cité des Sciences et de l'Industrie
Engineering Consultant: H.G.M.
Furniture Design: Gaëlle Lauriot-Prévost
Surface: 800 m² (total area): greenhouse (exhibition of plants) 400 m²,
exhibitions (scenographic elements) 400 m²
Cost: 5,600,000 FF (1996 value, before tax)
Program: Educational greenhouse; permanent scientific exhibition
of new methods of cultivation

The general scenery consists in creating a protected space "alongside the world", wherein a certain mystery reigns. Getting from the Great Greenhouse's surroundings to the Greenhouse itself is achieved through a lower antechamber encircled by the hand of a curtainlike draping of fabric.

The symbolic elements of information and consultation are brought together and organized between the greenhouse flooring and that of the Cité des Sciences et de l'Industrie. The detachment of the greenhouse thus offers two spaces, one for communication, the other for experimentation.

Continued

1   Study model
2&3 View of the greenhouse situated in the Cité des Sciences et de l'Industrie museum
4   Experimentation area on the first floor

1

2

3

4

In functional terms, this scheme encourages adaptation over a period of time. Such freedom of development favors the updating of the collection and the regulation of public access. The general scenery is ultimately linked to the functional consequences of this "magical" place, seeing that the Great Greenhouse is an instrument that must be able to regulate itself in space and time. For this reason the scenery takes the following main parameters into account:

• Access to the space is NATURAL: Continuity and fluidity of the visitor's movement, thanks to the detachment of the Great Greenhouse from the ground level.

• The place is MAGICAL: Autonomy of the experimental space as a living laboratory.

• The exhibition's identity is FACTUAL: The fabric enveloping the Greenhouse volume characterizes the exhibition space. This presence is amplified by the diffused light emanating from the Greenhouse itself.

• The technique is SIMPLE: The technical facilities are mainly installed in the ceiling of the Greenhouse, and allow for all the required interventions of adaptation and maintenance. The Greenhouse's flooring is a receptacle for draining the water, and forms a double watertight tank. The dissociation of the network constitutes the technical architecture of the system.

Previous page:
    Experimentation and crops on the first floor
6   Information desks on ground floor
Opposite:
    Gap between the "Batyline" cover and the glass façade

6

136

Book Technology Centre

Design/Completion 1993/1995
Industrial area Gustave Eiffel, 77600 Bussy Saint-Georges,
outskirts of Paris, France
Client: Bibliothèque nationale de France, Ministry of Education
and Research
Engineering Consultants: Séchaud & Bossuyt, T.P.S., H.G.M.
Monitoring: O.D.M.
Surface: Site area 65,300 m², building 25,000 m²,
possible extension 50,000 m²
Cost: 200,000,000 FF (1993 value, after tax)

The site of the Book Technology Centre
is located immediately alongside the A4
motorway and the A line of the regional
express rail link, which connects the new
town of Marne-la-Vallée to the center of
Paris in less than half an hour. The
Centre is a conservation tool shared by the
university libraries of the Paris region for
part of their collections of scientific
interest.

The buildings realized during the first
phase are organized along the western
edge of the site, so as to enable any future
extension to spread in three directions:
north, south and east. The compositional
axis of the overall plan is a covered indoor
street. Workshops and stores are organized
along this line of force. Arranged
perpendicularly to the north of the
covered indoor street, a series of parallel
buildings houses the workshops, offices,
conference rooms and classrooms. The
storage modules are located on the other
side of the indoor street.

The facades, 9 meters high for the
workshops and 15 meters high for the
storage blocks, are faced with aluminium
panels, some plain and others with
moveable slats. A kinetic effect is produced
by the alternation of these panels.

The indoor street has a glass roof, which
acts as a source of overhead lighting.

1

2

3

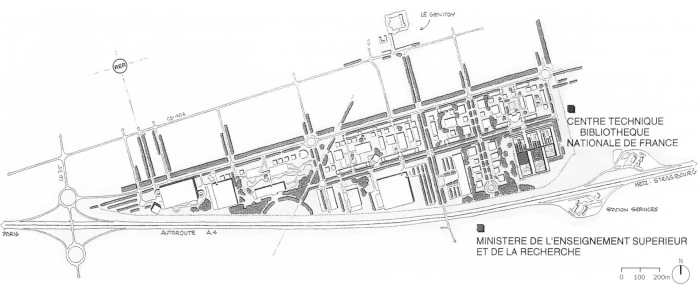

4

1   Delivery area

2&3   Façade of aluminium cladding

4   Site plan

5

7

6

8

8 View of interior street which organises the
   building's distribution
9 Under the delivery area cover
10–12 Schematic plans

9

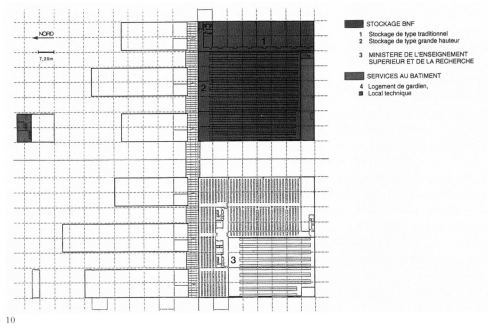

STOCKAGE BNF

1 Stockage de type traditionnel
2 Stockage de type grande hauteur

3 MINISTERE DE L'ENSEIGNEMENT
SUPERIEUR ET DE LA RECHERCHE

SERVICES AU BATIMENT

4 Logement de gardien,
■ Local technique

10

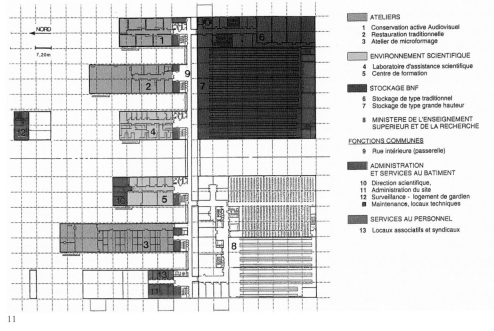

ATELIERS

1 Conservation active Audiovisuel
2 Restauration traditionnelle
3 Atelier de microformage

ENVIRONNEMENT SCIENTIFIQUE

4 Laboratoire d'assistance scientifique
5 Centre de formation

STOCKAGE BNF

6 Stockage de type traditionnel
7 Stockage de type grande hauteur

8 MINISTERE DE L'ENSEIGNEMENT
SUPERIEUR ET DE LA RECHERCHE

FONCTIONS COMMUNES

9 Rue intérieure (passerelle)

**ADMINISTRATION
ET SERVICES AU BATIMENT**

10 Direction scientifique,
11 Administration du site
12 Surveillance - logement de gardien
■ Maintenance, locaux techniques

SERVICES AU PERSONNEL

13 Locaux associatifs et syndicaux

11

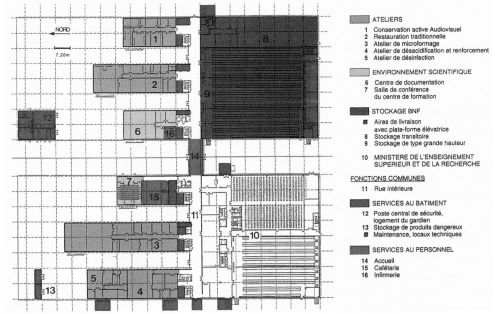

ATELIERS

1 Conservation active Audiovisuel
2 Restauration traditionnelle
3 Atelier de microformage
4 Atelier de désacidification et renforcement
5 Atelier de désinfection

ENVIRONNEMENT SCIENTIFIQUE

6 Centre de documentation
7 Salle de conférence
du centre de formation

STOCKAGE BNF

■ Aires de livraison
avec plate-forme élévatrice
8 Stockage transitoire
9 Stockage de type grande hauteur

10 MINISTERE DE L'ENSEIGNEMENT
SUPERIEUR ET DE LA RECHERCHE

FONCTIONS COMMUNES

11 Rue intérieure

SERVICES AU BATIMENT

12 Poste central de sécurité,
logement du gardien
13 Stockage de produits dangereux
■ Maintenance, locaux techniques

SERVICES AU PERSONNEL

14 Accueil
15 Cafétaria
16 Infirmerie

12

Lu Jia Zui Business District

Design Competition 1992, competition project
Pu Dong, City of Shanghai, China
Client: City of Shanghai
Surface: 4,000,000 m²
Architect's Mission: Urban development, development of the riverbanks
of the Pu Dong, development of the new business center of Shanghai
Architect's Activities: Analysis of the town planning (history and
geography), urban development scheme

The study for the development of a major business district in Shanghai, in the Lu Jia Zui district of Pu Dong, is one of the great planning reflections of our times. Our approach draws on the lessons of history, without excluding all the positive factors concerning the building of cities, whether they are ancient, modern or contemporary.

At the outset, it is necessary to perform a historic reading of the city's layout. This shows that Shanghai is defined by routes running from north to south and from east to west, forming a relatively orthogonal fabric. This factor determines the general orientation of the networks of the new district, so that it can be naturally linked to the existing city, and enables a comparison to be made with other cities that provide elements of reference, in order to assess the scope and needs of the project.

This historical and functional analysis of the city cannot, however, give an account of the symbolic dimension of the "founding event" that must inscribe the new district within the landscape of the city. This "founding event" must mark the development of the historic city center, of crossing over to the other bank, which generates a new identity for the "heart of Shanghai" by establishing another relationship between Town and Nature.

Opposite the river Bund, following its meander, we propose a broken line set at a right angle, facing from north to south and from east to west. This solitary and unique form is in counterpoint to the

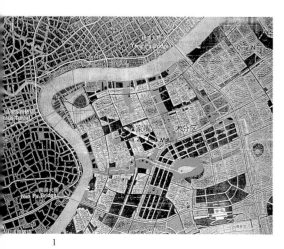

1

2

144

architecture on the other bank, like the *yin* and *yang*. It provides a great park at the water's edge, and its rosary of high-rises acts as a support for the development of Shanghai towards the east. Just like a furrow in a field, this set square traces the plan of the new town. There will be room for two million square metres of offices and areas of activity or commerce; beneath them there will be a road network for cars, carparks and two additional tunnels joining both banks.

The whole project is designed in terms of duration, of time passing, of the slow creation of our cities' landscapes. This research could be called "Towards a living urbanism", more interested in the void, the in-between, than in things themselves. We must protect the void; it is the city's most treasured possession. It enables the creation of places, it ensures the future of our cities, it guarantees the presence of nature. The void is immaterial, it is nothing, yet it constitutes "the foundation of our towns." All our relationships, our glances and our hopes, are established through the void.

1 Overall site plan
2 Planning scheme for the business district: presentation model
3 Traces, references, concepts, and analysis of the site

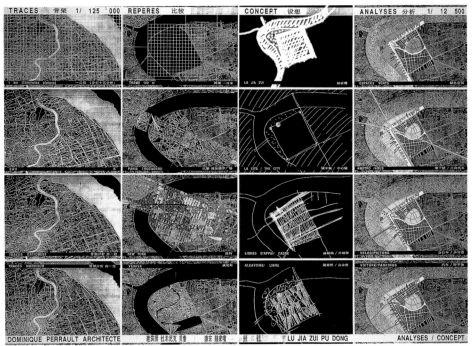

3

IRSID, Usinor-Sacilor Conference Center

Design/Completion 1989/1991, competition project–winner
"Chateau" de Saint Léger, 78105 Saint-Germain-en-Laye,
outskirts of Paris, France
Client: Usinor-Sacilor
Engineering Consultant: Setec Foulquier
Surface: 4,000 m²
Cost: 31,000,000 FF (1989 value, before tax)
Program: 200-seat auditorium, 12 conference rooms

Vis-à-vis the charm of the "chateau" and its "jewel-case of green", the addition or attachment of a new building seems contradictory, complicated and unsightly. In fact, what is called for is the revaluation and restoration of the existing building. In placing the chateau "on a glass plate," one creates a conspicuous place and a clearly-defined market.

This conspicuousness results from the tactful insertion of the new extension, which incorporates the lower part of the chateau into a glass volume that is set into the ground. The geometry of this circular base draws to it the many approaches that follow the main axis, the future entrance, and even the walkways at the far end of the park.

The glass disk filters the natural light and plays with the artificial light. This plate will, in effect, be smooth and shiny by day. The chateau will be reflected in it, as in a stretch of water. At nightfall, however, the effect will be the opposite, because the surface will be lit up, illuminating the chateau.

Continued

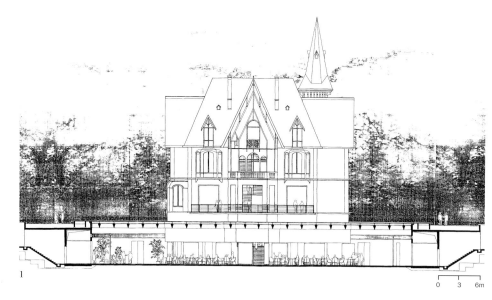

1

0 3 6m

2

1 Cross section
2 Model of the existing "château" on the glass disk,
   night view
Opposite:
   Existing "château" on the glass disk

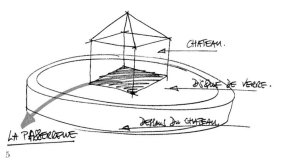

CHATEAU.

DISQUE DE VERRE.

DESSOUS DU CHATEAU.

LA PASSERELLE

4 Reflection of footpath in the glass disk
5 Sketch
6 Reflection of the existing "château" in the
glass disk

5

6

One could describe this project as a "glass and steel device", the reactions to which testify to the vitality of the building *qua* object, as well as to that of the surroundings. The spatial organization of the different functions is divided between "spaces for meeting," located in the chateau, and "spaces for communication," situated in the base. The whole structure is linked together by a stairway set at the center of the device.

The communications center is accessed through the chateau via a metal footbridge extending over the glass disk.

Seen in plan, a concentric system extends around the ancient building. In the central part, an area for services and corridors is located beneath the chateau; then comes a crown, which integrates the restaurant and auditorium; and finally, a technical ring groups the service entrances and emergency exits.

7   Aerial view of entrance footbridge and disk

7

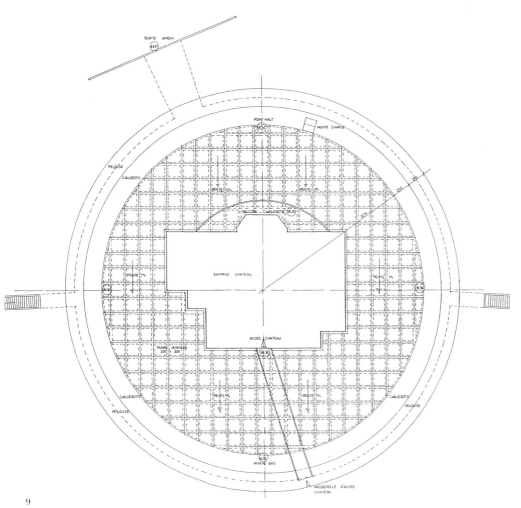

9

11

Opposite:
Reception room on the underground
level

9 Plan of the metal structure

10 Underground level

11 Glass disk reflections

10

IRSID, Usinor-Sacilor Conference Center   153

Archives for the Mayenne District in Laval

Design/Completion 1989/1993, competition project–winner
Rue des Archives, 53018 Laval, France
Client: Department of Mayenne
Construction Architect: Alfred Heude
Engineering Consultants: Séchaud & Bossuyt
Surface: 6,000 m²
Cost: 40,000,000 FF (1989 value, before tax)
Program: Extension of the archives to ensure a capacity up to the year 2040. Reading room, stockroom, auditorium, workshops, offices and independent house for director

The point of departure for this project is based on the volume of the building, thus rendering the installation of the storage systems both comprehensible and acceptable. In so doing, we have fitted out the old building for the functions of communication, and the (new) building is suited for the functions of conservation. The form of the building is a single volume covered in teak wood. The challenge of making a building of wood follows on from a desire to insert a candid type of architecture unobtrusively within a landscape. Around the project, the site is cleared to make it easier to set the edifice: a monument surrounded by a garden square. This urban development option lends the complex a quality of legibility with regard to its varous functions, affording both charm and nobility. The consultative function lies at the heart of the building, defined spatially by a large atrium that captures the natural light from the roof. The existing large windows are organized to frame views over the garden and the surrounding neighbourhood. The place is central. Around it are areas for specialized consultation and exhibitions. On the upper floors, similarly, the offices of the archival staff are arranged around the empty space of the atrium.

At the very top of this arrangement, a conference room doubles as a place for research and communications. We were keen to use the existing heritage to develop a project that would be an example of permanence and change alike – the solid nature of stone, the warmth of wood – and would lend itself easily to the extension planned for completion by the year 2040.

2

1

154

4

5

1 The archives reading room
2 Existing refurbished building and new extension
3 Detail of the new extension façade
4 New extension façade (storage building)
5 Reading room with metal mesh ceiling

Ecole nationale des Ponts et Chaussées

Design 1989, Competition project
Ecole nationale Superieure de Geographie/ENPC/ENSG
Marne-la-Vallée, France
Client: Minister of Equipment
Surface: 40,354 m²
Associate Architects: Bruno Laudat, Catherine Hass, Antoine Canet
Program: classrooms, laboratory, administration

The engineer of the 21st century is no longer a rough technician; he or she is aware and respectful of the need to maintain the balance between the natural surroundings and the human environment.

The site on which this school is built gives the impression of a case of greenery, a clearing surrounded by woods and wonderfull species.

The project valorizes this privileged site through a "large shelter" of glass, housing schools and their shared amenities within a garden. The concept of nature wrapped in a glass-and-metal skin stages a functional mode that is more free and more open to the outside world. The gardens constitute a natural extension of the surroundings.

The school is a representation of the contemporary world, mingling its differences and inventing novel group identities.

The global enveloping around the building's long-limbs, which are spread out in the garden, provides a unity of its different functions and internal uses.

Freedom of organization is directly proportional to imaginative capacity.

1 2

3

1&2 Presentation model: overall view
  3 Elevations
4–7 Presentation model with metal mesh roof cover
     structure

156

4

5

6

7

Headquarters for Canal + TV Channel

Design 1988, with distinction from jury, competition project—highly commended

Quai André Citroën/rue des Cevennes/rue Balard, 15th Arrondissement, Paris, France

Client: Cogedim Aménagement

Surface: 22,500 m²

Program: Offices, stages, studios, administration, parking, workshops and restaurant

The fact that it occupies a site facing the river Seine gives this building an excellent position. We proposed to "appropriate" the nearby garden to bring its presence into the building by prolonging this green space into the ground level. In this way, we obtained a block of green on which the new headquarters would lie and be integrated.

This building, a glass parallelepiped, finds its urban dimension through its radiant and shiny appearance. It is a glass that lies on a garden, which shines during the daytime and sparkles at night. In terms of communication, our aim was to open to the city the activity of the headquarters of a large television channel.

The materials are glass-type, transparent, translucent, etc., following the functional requirements and aesthetics issues. The structure is of stainless steel and aluminium. The floors are covered mainly in wood, with fitted carpet in the service spaces. Concerning the garden, we can imagine prolonging the exterior garden, combining stone and green surfaces.

In conclusion, the building is a witness of its time, gathering together architecture and nature, a building working with efficiency, accentuating natural light, opening itself to the outside world, in a word, a certain idea of liberty.

1 Site plan
2 Presentation model

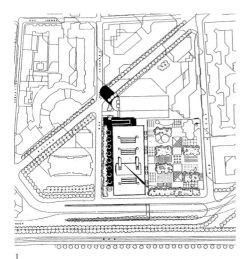

1

2

3

4

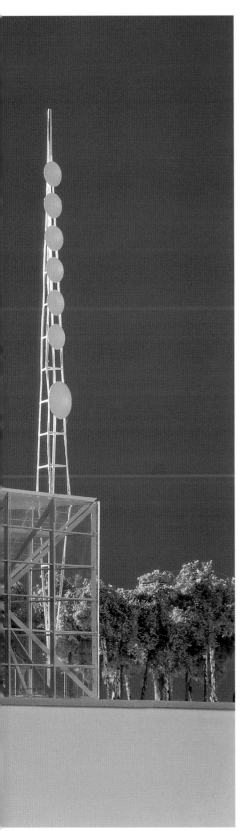

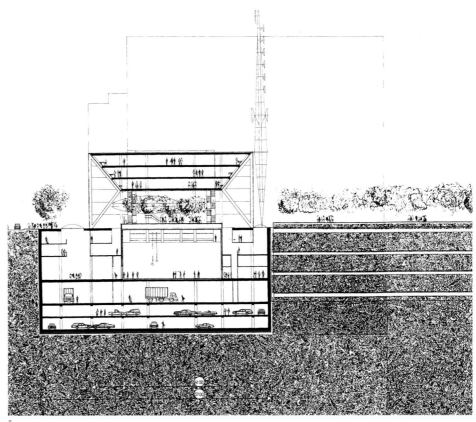

5

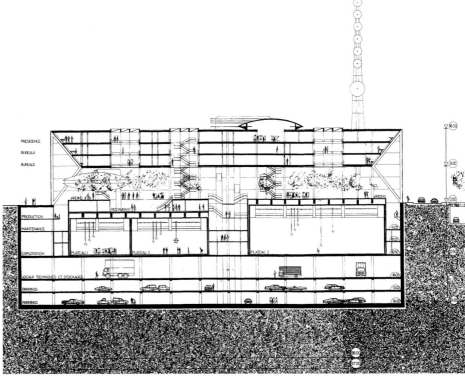

6

Water Purification Plant for S.A.G.E.P.

Design/Completion 1987/1993, competition project–winner
33 Avenue Jean Jaures, 94200 Ivry-sur-Seine,
Metropolitan Area of Paris, France
Client: S.A.G.E.P. (Société Anonyme de Gestion des Eaux de Paris)
Engineering Consultants: OTV/Dogremont, SETEC Foulquier
Surface: 9 ha (total area): offices (1,900 m^2)
Cost: 500,000,000 FF (1993 value, before tax with technical equipment)
Architect's Mission: Modernization of the water treatment plant in Ivry-sur-Seine, which supplies Paris with drinking water; development of the site
Program: Offices, laboratories, and workshops

This project involved "cladding" rather than designing. With the exception of the relationship with the Avenue Jean-Jaures (a 200 metres linear disposition to Ivry), the remainder of the land acquired for the plant – some 9 hectares on the banks of the Seine – is strictly invisible and out of bounds to the public. *A priori*, the challenge of the plant's architectural image is thus of little importance, and it is more a matter of conceiving an internal landscape, and providing the best possible working conditions. The operation thus entails, first and foremost, the siting and setting of the plant, in terms of colour and light, covering all the technical systems of the site. The sole and more classical architectural reference is a slender building housing laboratories and offices, set on piles in the middle of the site and beside the treatment ponds. The most spectacular feature is perhaps the idea of a peripheral cowling, like a large rectangular and transparent buoy 8 metres high.

Continued

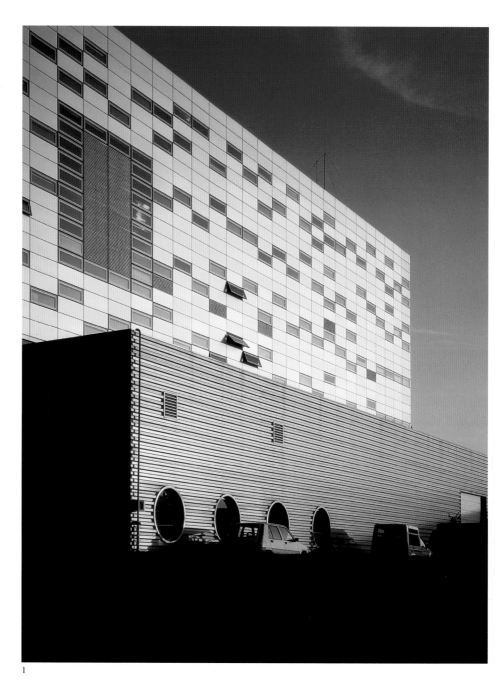

1

1   Façade of offices and laboratory buildings
2&3   Water reservoir and treatment plant

It is this glass and metal cylinder, rising over the Avenue Jean-Jaures, that now forms the façade of the plant facing the town. Behind the glassed curves are the technical appliances of a maintenance hall, an idea that takes the staff out of dank basements. The prospect offered by these long cylinders, 200 metres in length, and punctuated by markers on the ground and pipes, is a striking one. A film set, no less, bathed in grey paint, and rough or gritty concrete, and extended terrace-like by expanses of water. The building housing the laboratories and offices is set in the midst of this landscape. It is a smooth, slender object, whose aluminium façade is punctuated by a series of random horizontal openings. A stairway sheathed in grey lattice-work, like an oblique airport airlock, connects the plant to a small building. Near the old pump building, Dominique Perrault has once again created a "technical garden", turning tanks into totems, placing pumps on stands behind windows, and playing with the features of the plant.

4   Façade cladding of offices and laboratory
     buildings
5&6 Water treatment reservoir and factory

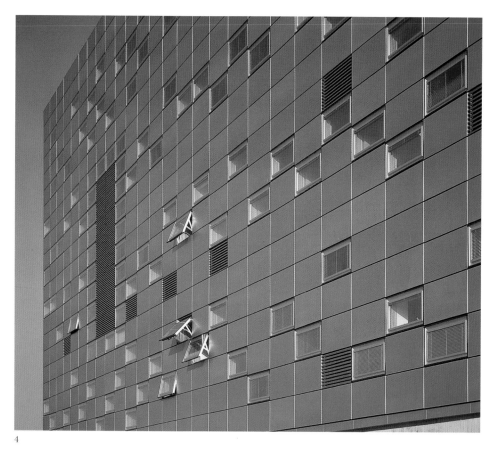

4

6

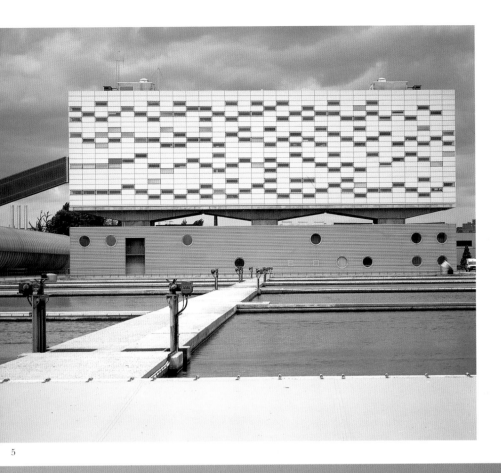

5

7

8

9

7 Water treatment reservoir
8 The factory's curved cladding during construction
9 Water treatment plant against the suburbs of Paris

10&11   Interior view of the factory's gallery in
         relationship with the Avenue Jean-Jaures
Opposite:
         Staircase connection between factory and
         offices and laboratories

10

11

Hôtel Industriel Jean-Baptiste Berlier

Design/Completion 1986/1990, competition project–winner
26/34 Rue Bruneseau, 75013 Paris, France
Client: S.A.G.I. (Société Anonyme de Gestion Immobilière)
Engineering Consultants: Technip and Planitec
Surface: 21,000 m²
Cost: 72,000,000 FF (1986 value, before tax)
Program: Building for light industry workshops and offices (9 floors), staff canteen, and parking (basement)
Constructa Preis '92 (European Prize for Industrial Architecture)

Architecture is not an art of exclusion

Five years ago, in the 13th arrondissement, the City of Paris, together with the Société Anonyme de Gestion Immobilière, launched an urban architectural competition to try and see what could be done with "that bit of land" trapped between the bypass cloverleaf, the Quai d'Ivry, and the bundle of tracks of the Gare d'Austerlitz.

As if the site did not leave it unaffected, the brief proposed, in its own way, the implementation of an abstraction, "an industrial HQ," a new type of building that was neither offices nor industrial premises, simply an "intelligent" space, housing occupants with a wide range of different activities whose evolution could not be foreseen; WHITE SQUARE ON WHITE BACKGROUND. Nothing, less than nothing, no footing, no hold, no hook, no soothing theories about the city-with-parks-and-gardens, but a confrontation with "our world," the one out there, the real, so-called "tough" world, the one we pretend we don't want, the one we've come to terms with; in fact, a "softly spoken" contemporary cityscape with road haulage depots, motorways, rubbish-incineration plants, a cement manufacturer's silo, a helicopter pad for medical emergencies, a traffic control and maintenance center for the 250,000 vehicles driving each day on the bypass. Let's stop thinking about the existence of such BLIGHTED PLACES and absorb their energy instead, right where

1

1　Night view of the main entrance façade
2　The Hôtel Industriel Jean-Baptiste Berlier,
　surrounded by the city's road networks
3　View across the railway site

2

3

it's given off. Let's bring another vision to this ceaseless traffic of trundling, flying objects, the city's perpetual motion, and go on bringing to it a "certain something," a *je ne sais quoi* which, with "the best will in the world," will provide evidence of the place's transfiguration. Let's get on with it, then – plant ourselves bang in the middle of the site, in full view of this fantastic spectacle of urbanity. To get the most out of it, let's work, bathed in a natural light picked up by a GLASS BOX, surround ourselves with all kinds of services, comfort at all levels, networks, connections, in order to be able to adapt to changing ways of life and modes of production. Contained in this glass brick will be forty or so businesses employing five hundred people; some of these businesses will flourish, others disappear, the building will not remain indifferent to these changes, the evolution of its activities will always be visible up front, and that will be the expression of its reality.

To live happily, let's not live in hiding. It's not a question of constructing a historic building, an eco-museum on hold, but a living system vibrant with the shockwaves of its present environment, because this object is there, and not elsewhere.

5

6

University for Electrical and Electronic Engineering

Design/Completion 1984/1987, competition project–winner
Cité Descartes, Marne-la-Vallée, Metropolitan Area of Paris, France
Client: Chamber for Commerce and Industry (CCI)
Engineering Consultants: B.E.F.S. TEC/Planitec
Surface: 40,000 m²
Cost: 160,000,000 FF (1984 value, before tax)
Program: Institute for 1100 students in 1991, library, amphitheater, canteen for students and kitchen, laboratories, workshops, and gymnasium

The Cité Descartes, which is situated between the first and second sectors of the new town of Marne-la-Vallée, has been intentionally planned and conceived as a prestigious focal point of technology. It accommodates well known and well reputed public organizations and private concerns alike, in a lush green landscape with plenty of trails and densely wooded areas. Starting from this premise, the architecture must not only comply with the various spaces and places, but it must also endow each leaseholder and purchaser with a specific corporate image.

The University for Electrical and Electronic Engineering (ESIEE) occupies a key position in the layout of the city. At the far end of the large public place, the building, by being triangular, offers a new skyline, akin to a backdrop that has no end.

1

2

1 Night view of restaurant terrace
2 East façade
3 Entrance
4 Aerial view
5 Ground floor
6 Interior street

3

4

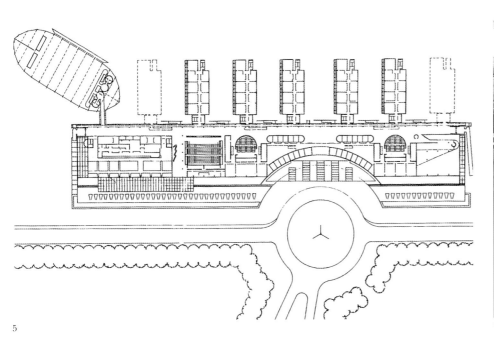

5

6

By being handled like a huge plane set at an angle over its 300-metre length, it offers a metaphor for taking flight. Instead of enhancing the street with a vertical façade, the architect has chosen to sidestep the frontal aspect. The slant makes it easier to have an overall perception of the school. The form of the ESIEE is far from being a pure cliché of some contemporary mythology. Rather, it is the expression of its essence and its destination. The · building is part and parcel of the "newlands" of the Ile-de-France; it takes part in the movement of land acquisition that is gathering momentum to the east of Paris. The architect takes pleasure in letting it be known that the developer chose the site in a helicopter. From that starting point, it is the act of foundation by projection that is emphasized.

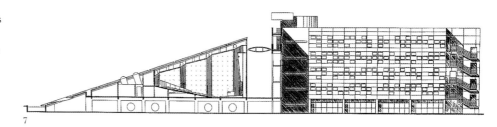

7

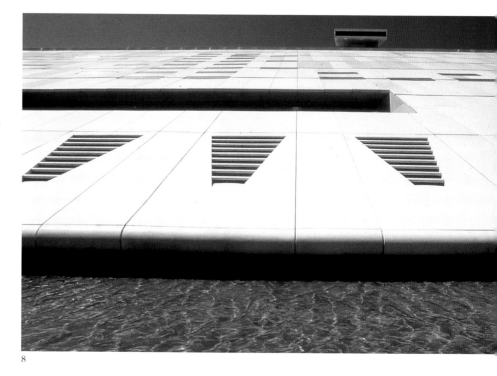

8

7   Cross section
8   Cladding detail of the façade-roof
9   Courtyard between two classroom buildings
10   Gymnasium
11   Restaurant
12   Gymnasium

9

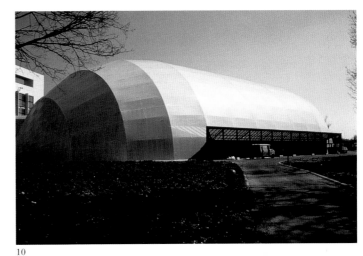

10

11

12

Olympic Velodrome and Swimming Pool

Design/Completion 1992/September 1997 (Radsporthalle), November 1999 (Schwimmsporthalle), competition project–winner

Landsberger Allee, Berlin, Germany

Client: City of Berlin, Department for Construction and Housing, represented by Olympia 2000 Sportstattenbauten GmbH (OSB)

Second Prize of the Deutscher Architekturpreis 1999

Construction and Development Associate Architects: APP Berlin (Dominique Perrault, Rolf Reichert Architect R.P.M., and Schmidt-Schicketanz und Partner)

Engineering: Ove Arup and Partners

Landscape: Lanschaft Planen & Bauen, Berlin

This project is bound up with the reunification of the two Germanies. It was related to the wish of a city, Berlin, then about to become the capital, to be nominated for the Olympic Games in the year 2000. From the first, there was a conjunction of the political ambitions of the Berlin Senate, an extremely strong desire for the redeployment and linking together of the two parts of the city, and a unifying project, the Olympic project, that enabled the planners to develop not only the setting up of a certain number of sporting facilities, but also a certain number of networks to serve these sporting facilities. It is within this context, at once enthusiastic and contentious, that the city of Berlin set up an international competition for the design of the Olympic velodrome and swimming pool. The site chosen is at the intersection of two important urban elements: a major axis that goes from the city center (from Alexander Platz in the direction of Moscow), a wide avenue, which subsequently meets a second element, a peripheral one, namely a short metro line, which has since linked east and west, and which enables a tour of the city to be made.

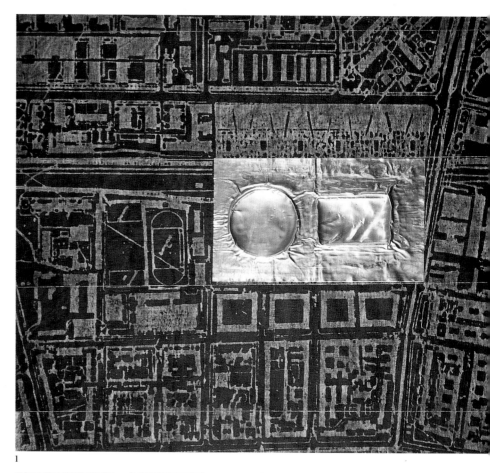

1

2

3

Monitoring: Projecktmanagement Olympiasportstatten (Promos)

Cycle Track: Herbert and Ralph Schurmann Architects

Sports Planning Dept: Weidleplan Consulting GmbH, F. Kerschkamp

Surface: 100,000 m²

Cost: 550,000,000 DM (1992 value, after tax)

Construction Period: Velodrome, 3 years; swimming hall, 3 years

Program: Sports complex in a landscape (park). Swimming hall: 4,000 spectators, 2 Olympic pools, 1 diving pool. Velodrome: 9,000 spectators

Multifunctional Use of the Velodrome: Cycling, athletics, tennis, physical education, horse riding, concerts

1 Conceptual model
2 Aerial view, computer drawing (swimming pool at the first plan)
3 Aerial view, constructed project (velodrome at the first plan)
4 View from the office of D. Perrault in winter
5 Velodrome roof detail

The intersection of different networks, then... But also the intersection of fabrics... The concave part of the system contains an ensemble of fabrics typical of the standard Berliner block, plus the presence of the former Berlin abattoirs; and on the other hand, we find, on the far side of the railway track, 20 km given over to extended, slab-type blocks of flats; a completely different type of urbanism, then.

In order to resolve the conjunction of these two systems, we decided, in a somewhat obvious experiment, to cause the two buildings that house the Olympic swimming pool and velodrome to vanish from sight.

The concept here is limited to the considerations of a rectangular, quadrilateral territory on which two forms are inscribed; a round shape for the velodrome and a rectangular one for the swimming pool. The question of the form being thus resolved, done away with, we were able to address other issues... There are many things to stitch back together in this neighborhood, many things to link up, and neither the time nor the place appeared to lend itself to the reception, the welcoming of a volume (or two volumes) of this size, which would, in my opinion, have curtailed exchanges between the different areas, rather than uniting and developing them...

Continued

4

5

Just as the Bibliothèque nationale de France offers Paris a large public space, it seemed interesting to me that the design of these two enormous buildings would provide an opportunity for the design of the city.

Our experience in weaving urban fabrics has often been based on the siting of a public space, and in this instance in Berlin, in the siting of a verdant public space.

The urban concept behind this project is the creation of a green space on a handsome scale (approximately 200 ¥ 500 meters), and at the center of this green space to implant… buildings, shall we say. Berlin is highly interesting from the geographical and landscape point of view, because it is almost a suburban space intimately linked to a city that has every claim to its noble rank. In Berlin one finds a way of blending nature and architecture. And this blending of nature and architecture is, as I see it, a form of intervention, of a work that can be developed in the city…

Continued

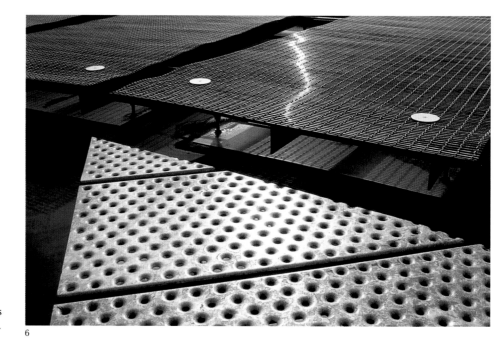

6

7

11

12

and particularly in Berlin. This didn't mean creating the umpteenth public park... Since there are already many of these, it meant finding a definition for this park that would be appropriate to the neighborhood while being different to the others, yet also relate to this natural presence at the heart of the area. Our idea was to create an orchard. Namely, to plant apple trees. The idea is that when you approach on foot through this orchard you discover, set into the ground and sticking out at a height of about a meter, two tables... One round and the other rectangular, covered with a wire gauze. These two metal surfaces will shimmer in the sunlight and appear, at first sight, to be stretches of water more than buildings, rather like lakes at the center of the orchard. To do this, and before speaking of buildings, the trees will have to be

Continued

13

procured! We tried to find – in Germany, but also in France – apple trees that were, so to speak, already the bearers of a certain history. A little over 400, say 450, apple trees have been planted, and they must bear the traces of their past, so that we get the feeling that this orchard has been here for a certain time.

It just so happens that when you try and buy fruit trees of a certain size, around 35 years old, it becomes rather interesting from the financial viewpoint, because the tree has already paid its way. That's why you can find, particularly in Normandy, splendid apple trees at very competitive prices, which allowed us to propose transplanting such trees. To compare a German apple tree and a French apple tree is a bit like comparing a French cheese to a German cheese... On the one hand you have a farmhouse cheese, and on the other a pasteurized one...

Continued

14   15

186

16

17

German apple trees are very fine, extremely upright and well put together, but they are rather uniform in kind, the product of a particular sort of production, at least in terms of their bearing. And that didn't suit us. It wasn't enough just to find these trees, it was also important to be sure they'd first resist being transported, but above all that they'd then cope with being transplanted; that is, adapt to their Berlin life and its winters… If I had to do things all over again, I'd probably concern myself more with trees than with buildings, because I've met people involved with trees who remain passionate about what they do (which isn't necessarily our everyday environment), and on top of that there's a really moving relationship with the living world which enables you to glimpse other ways of being, and maybe even certain ways of being that are currently beyond our ken.

19

20

19 Aerial view from the surrounding building, swimming pool
on the first plan
20 Roof detail
21 Vestiaries
22 Entertainment swimming pool with olympic measurements

21

22

23

23   Diving pool
Opposite:
    Main Olympic pool

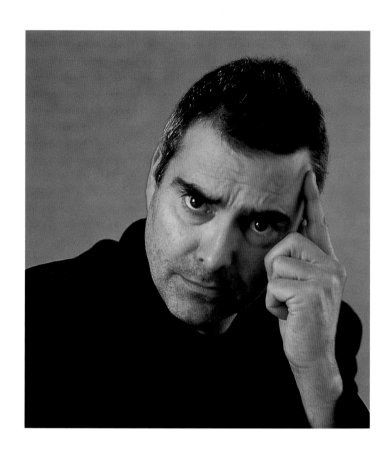

Biography

Dominique Perrault

Born: 9 April 1953

Profession: Architect qualified by the Government (DPLG)–
Urban Planner by the French Society of Urban Planners (SFU)

Address: 26 rue Bruneseau,   and Paul-Heyse-Straße 29
F–75629 Paris cédex 13   D–10407 Berlin

Phone: +33 (0) 144 06 00 00   Phone: +49 (30) 421 03 500
Fax: +33 (0) 144 06 00 01   Fax: +49 (30) 421 03 502

E-mail: dparchi@club-internet.fr

Selected Awards and Memberships

Great National Prize of Architecture (1993)

Mies van der Rohe Pavilion Award for European Architecture,
conferred by the Foundation Mies van der Rohe and the
European Parliament, for the Bibliothèque nationale de France
(French National Library) (1997)

Chevalier of the Legion of Honour (January 1997)

Honorable member of the Association of German Architects
(BDA)

Member of the Academy of Architecture

President of the French Institute of Architecture (Institut Français
d'Architecture, IFA) since 1998

University Graduations

1978 Diploma in Architecture (Ecole Nationale
Supérieure des Beaux-Arts de Paris)

1979 Higher Diploma in Town Planning (Ecole Supérieure
des Ponts et Chaussée, Paris)

1980 Postgraduate degree in history (Ecole des Hautes
Etudes en Sciences Sociales, Paris)

Office Openings

1981 Paris office

1992 Berlin office

1998 Luxembourg office

Professorships

1995–96 School of Architecture, Rennes, France

1997 School of Architecture, New Orleans, USA

1998 Urbana–Champaign, Chicago, USA

1999 Escola Tècnica Superior d'Arquitectura
de Barcelona, Spain

2000 Institut Victor Horta, Brussels, Belgium

2001 Eidgenösische Technische Hochschule (ETH),
Zurich, Switzerland

Missions in France And Abroad

1982–84 Development architect in the Parisian town
planning workshop (APUR)

1986 Consultant architect for the Loiret department
council

1988–98 Member of the board of the French Institute of
Architecture (IFA)

1990–92 Consultant architect for the city of Nantes, France

1992–96 Consultant architect for the city of Bordeaux,
France

1994–1997 Member of the council for urban planning of the
city of Salzburg, Austria

1996 Member of the jury of EUROPAN 4, Graz, Austria

1997–98 President of the jury of the French Academy in
Rome, Italy (Villa Medicis)

1998 Member of the jury of EUROPAN 5, Helsinki,
Finland

1998 Member of the jury for the Mies van der Rohe
Award

2000 Member of the Urbanism Committee of Barcelona,
Spain

2000 President of the jury, Fukushima, Japan

2000 Member of the jury, Mies van der Rohe Award for
Central America

2000 President of the French Institute of Architecture
(IFA) since 1998

Staff List

Dominique Perrault, Architect-Planner
Aude Perrault, Architect, Financial Manager
Gaelle Lauriot-Prevost, Architect, Design and Artistic Manager

Rolf Reichert, Associate architect in Germany
Paczowski & Fritsch, Associate architect in Luxembourg
Luca Bergo, Associate architect in Italy
Joan Carles Navarro & Albert Salazar, associate architects in Spain

Technical specialists

Guy Morisseau, ECAM, Engineer and Technical Manager.

Fabrice Bougon, Construction Economist

Jean-Paul Lamoureux, Acoustic Engineer

Erik Jacobsen, Agronomist engineer and Landscape designer

Team in Paris

Architects

Constantino Coursaris, RIBA

Ralf Lavedag, Dipl.Ing.

Natalie Plagaro-Cowee, ETSAM

Mathias Fritsch, DPLG

Cyril Lancelin, DPLG

Jérôme Thibault

Moreno Maconi, Dipl. Arch. ETH.

Anne Speicher, Dipl.Ing.

Thomas Barra, Dipl.Ing.

Severine De Love, DPLG

Eve Deprez, DPLG

Katrin Thornauer, Dipl.Ing.

Guilhem Menanteau, Engineer ECL, Politecnico de Milano

Trainees

Helen Brotschi

Yoel Karaso

Shigeki Maeda

Francesca Rezzonico

Three-dimensional representation

Michel Goudin – models

Didier Ghislain – perspectives

Secretary and administration

Luciano d'Aliesio

Awards & Exhibitions

Awards

1983 Winner, "Programme for New Architecture" (PAN XII)

1983 Winner, "Album of Young Architecture," Ministry of Housing

1984 First prize, AMO (architect/client) for Someloire tool plant

1990 Second prize, town planning for Bibliothèque nationale de France

1990 First prize, *Moniteur* magazine, for Hôtel Industriel Jean-Baptiste Berlier (Equerre d'Argent)

1990 First prize, AMO (architect/client) for Hôtel Industriel Jean-Baptiste Berlier

1992 Constructa Prize '92, European prize for Hôtel Industriel Jean-Baptiste Berlier

1993 Great National Architecture Prize (Grand prix national d'architecture)

1996 Special mention, Constructec-Prize 1996 (European prize for industrial architecture) for the SAGEP Water Purification Plant

1997 Mies van der Rohe Pavilion Award for European Architecture, conferred by the Foundation Mies van der Rohe and the European Parliament, for the Bibliothèque nationale de France (French National Library)

1999 German Award of Architecture (second prize), for the Berlin Olympic velodrome and swimming pool

Exhibitions

1991 Gallery Denise René / Rive Gauche, Paris, France, "Studies for the Bibliothèque de France"

1991 Gallery Denise René / Rive Droite, Paris, France, "Concept–Context"

1992 French Institute of Architecture (IFA), Paris, France, monographic exhibition

1994 Bordeaux, France, Monographic exhibition (Arc en Rêve), exhibition and public presentation of urban study,

1996 Aedes Gallery, Berlin, Germany

1996 Architekturgalerie, Luzern, Switzerland

1996 Biennale, Venice, Italy

1996 Netherlands Architecture Institute, Rotterdam, The Netherlands, "Europe in dialogue"

1997 Museum of Contemporary Art, Barcelona, Spain, "New Landscapes"

1997 GA Gallery, Tokyo, Japan, "The Six French Architects"

1997 Portuguese Architecture Institute, Lisbon, Portugal, monographic exhibition

1998 Architekturforum Innsbruck, Innsbruck, Germany, monographic exhibition

May 1998 IFA, Paris, France, Fifth Mies van der Rohe Award 1997 exhibition

Sep 1998 Copenhagen, Denmark, monographic exhibition

Nov 1998 TN Probe Gallery, Tokyo, Japan, monographic exhibition

Jan 1999 Ministerio de Fomento, Madrid,.Spain, monographic exhibition

Nov 1999 Gammel Dok, Copenhagen, Denmark, monographic exhibition

Nov 1999 Tallinn, Estonia, monographic exhibition

Jan 2000 Finnish Museum of Architecture, Helsinki, Finland, monographic exhibition

National and International Competitions

2000

January	Offices for Worldwide Intellectual Property Organisation,Geneva, Switzerland
March	Stone Cutters Bridge, Hong Kong, China
April	Extension of the Modern Art Gallery, Rome, Italy
July	New Headquarters for Danish Broadcasting, Copenhagen, Denmark
August	Urbanism studies, Las Teresitas, Tenerife, Spain

1999

January	Town Hall, district of Marseille, France
January	French Pavillon for the Hanover 2000 International Exhibition, Hanover, Germany
March	Congress Center, Graz, Austria
May	Railway station hall and buffet development, Blois, France
May	MesseHalle, Stuttgart, Germany
June	Casa dà Musica, Porto, Portugal
June	Offices for the Palais de Justice, Salerno, Italy
July	City of Gallega Culture, Santiago de Compostela, Spain
September	"Tower Schemes," Tower of London development, London, England
November	René Thys sport complex, Rheims, France
December	Consiag Offices, Prato, Italy
December	Ski Jump, Innsbruck, Austria
December	Luminous signals' design, Milan, Italy
December	Extension of the Reina Sofia Museum, Madrid, Spain (second prize)

1998

January	Exhibition site and service center, Basel, Switzerland
January	Site of the Montparnasse Tower, Paris, France (consulting)
March	Lehrter Bahnhof Tower, Berlin, Germany
April	Maritime Station "Môle de la Joliette," Marseille, France

May	New headquarters of the Institute of Architecture,Venice, Italy
June	Scenographic exhibition TOPKAPI: Treasures of the Sultan, Castle of Versailles, France
September	Footbridge, Parc de Bercy-Tolbiac, Paris, France
September	Central market redevelopment, Nancy, France
September	Fitting out, arranging, Temple of Mitra, Naples, Italy
October	Redevelopment of the FALCK site, Sesto San Giovanni, Milan, Italy
October	4-star Hotel, Nahuel Huapi National Park, Argentina
October	EUR Convention Center, Rome, Italy
December	Anti-noise Walls concept for the French Infrastructure Department, France

1997

January	Town Hall, shops and hotel, Innsbruck, Austria (winning project)
January	French Embassy, Berlin, Germany
January	Departmental Archives in Annecy, Haute-Savoie, France
March	Extension to the Museum of Modern Art (MOMA), New York, USA
June	Refurbishment and extension of "Cargo" cultural centre, Grenoble, France
September	Costantini Museum, Buenos Aires, Argentina (private contracting authority)
September	Olympic village, Kitzbühel, Austria
October	Central Media Library, Vénissieux (near Lyon), France, (winning project)
November	Urban development in connection with new tramway, Bordeaux, France

1996

March	Foreign Office Department, Berlin, Germany
May	Archives Centre, Rheims, France
June	National Library Kansai-Kan, Kyoto, Japan

June	Great Extension of the Court of Justice of the European Community, Luxembourg (with associated architects Paczowski & Fritsch)
August	Airport of Dortmund, Germany
September	Theatre (500 seats) in Château Gontier, France
October	Design of city lightings for the City of Paris, France
December	European centre of Federal Express (administration and transport), Roissy–Charles de Gaulle Airport, France

1995

January	Yokohama Harbour, Yokohama, Japan (mentioned project)
February	Very high-tensile pylon design, Electricité de France
April	A20 motorway, Brive-Montauban, France, for Autoroutes du Sud de la France
April	Town centre redevelopment, urban studies, Tremblay-en-France, France (winning project)
June	Nations' Place, Republic and Geneva Canton, urban studies (Following the competition, Dominique Perrault is chosen to build Geneva's Security Policy Centre)
June	The Great Greenhouse, Cité des Sciences et de l'Industrie, Paris, France (winning project)
July	Extension of velodrome stadium, Marseilles, France
October	Exit for Berlin underground (Torhäuser, Leipziger Platz), Berlin, Germany
October	Building of the Ministry of Culture, rue Saint-Honoré, Paris
November	Pre-landscaping and Redevelopment of the UNIMETAL Site, District du Grand Caen, France (winning project)

1994

November	Neptune Water Purification Plant, "Petite Californie", Nantes, France

Publications

1988   *ESIEE*, photographs, Hubert Tonka and Georges Fessy, Editions du demi-cercle, France (out of print)

1990   *Hôtel industriel Berlier*, photographs, Hubert Tonka and Georges Fessy, Editions du demi-cercle, Paris France (out of print)

1994   *Monography*, Artémis editions, Zürich, Switzerland

1995   *La Bibliothèque nationale de France*, Birkhäuser editions, Bâle, Switzerland

1996   Exhibition catalogue for the Aedes Gallery, edited by Sens & Tonka, Berlin, Germany

1996   Exhibition catalogue *Des Natures*, Architekturgalerie Luzern, Birkhäuser editions, Bâle, Switzerland

1997   *Meubles et Tapisseries, Furniture and Fabrics*, Birkhäuser editions, Bâle, Switzerland (Basel/Boston/Berlin: Birkhäuser–publishers for architecture)

1998   *Petits projets*, Gili editions, Barcelona, Spain

1998   Exhibition catalogue, edited by TN Probe, Tokyo, Japan

1998   Exhibition catalogue, edited by E. Messerschmidt and G. Hansen, Copenhagen, Denmark

1998   *L'Hôpital du livre, Centre technique de la Bibliothèque nationale de France*, Sens & Tonka, edition, Paris, France

1999   Monograph, Actar / Birkhäuser editions, Bâle, Switzerland

1999   *APLIX*, Lars Müller editions, Baden, Switzerland

2000   *Claude Rutault*, exhibition catalogue for Claude Rutault's installation in the Hôtel Industriel Jean-Baptiste Berlier, Paris, France

2000   *Dominique Perrault*, The Master Architect series, Images Publishing Group, Melbourne, Australia

2000   Monograph, Electa Editions, Milan, Italy, to be issued

2000   *Olympic Velodrome and Swimming Pool*, Actar editions, Barcelona, Spain, to be issued

Filmography

1995   *L'arbre, le livre et l'architecte*, directed by Richard Copans, produced by Les Films d'Ici, Bibliothèque nationale de France and Perrault Projets, Paris, France

1998   *Caen, le grand plateau; Hôtel industriel Jean-Baptiste Berlier; Bibliothèque nationale de France; Berlin, Vélodrome olympique*, "Architectures de Dominique Perrault" series, directed by Richard Copans, produced by Les Films d'Ici and Perrault Projets, Paris, France

1999   *Dominique Perrault*, "Les mots de l'architecte" series, directed by Richard Copans, produced by Les Films d'ici and Paris Première, Paris, France

Chronological List of Buildings & Projects

*Indicates work featured in this book

2000	**Greenhouse for the Museum of Natural History,**
	Arboretum of Chevreloup, Versailles, France

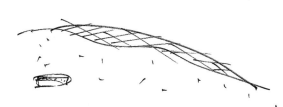

New Headquarters for Danish Broadcasting
Copenhagen, Denmark

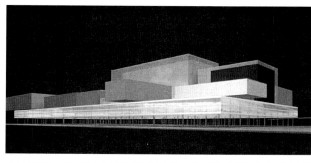

Extension to the Gallery of Modern Art
Rome, Italy

Stonecutters Bridge
Hong Kong, China

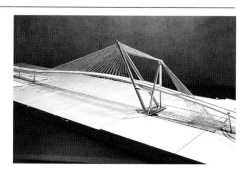

Offices for OMPI
Geneva, Switzerland

Design of an Illuminated Sign
Milan, Italy

1999 **Hotel tower for Grupo Habitat**
Barcelona, Spain

M-Preis Supermarket
Wattens, Austria

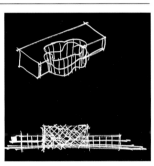

Urban Installation for the City of Bretigny
Brétigny sur Orge, France

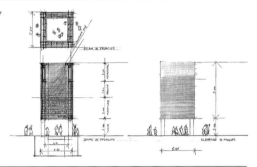

Domotex Fair
Hanover, Germany

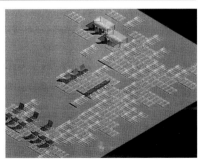

Ski Jump
Innsbruck, Austria

Consiag Offices
Prato, Italy

Sports Complex
Rheims, France

Urban Planning and Services Design
London, England

Extension to the Reina Sofia Museum
Madrid, Spain

Restructuring of the Cognacq-Jay Hospital
Paris, France

City of Culture
St. Jacques de Compostel, Spain

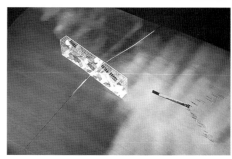

Offices for the Palais de Justice in Salerne
Salerno, Italy

Hall of Music
Porto, Portugal

Exhibition Centre
Stuttgart, Germany

Development of the Hall and Buffet of Blois Railway Station
Blois, France

Conference Centre
Graz, Austria

Conception of the French Pavilion for Expo 2000
Hanover, Germany

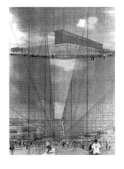

Redevelopment of the Town Hall Site
Marseille, France

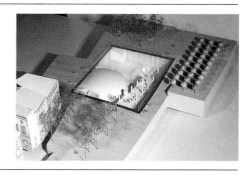

1998   **Anti-noise Walls**
Autoroutes France

Study of the Central Media Library Quarter
Vénissieux, France

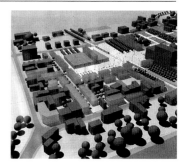

**Furniture and Household Objects
in Metal and Metal Mesh**

**Study for Cablecar between City Centre
and the Kirchberg Plateau**
Luxembourg

*Eur Convention Center
Rome, Italy

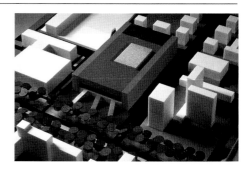

4-star Hotel
Nahuel Huapi National Park, Argentina

***Redevelopment of the Falck Site**
Sesto San Giovanni, Milan, Italy

*Pfleiderer Stand
Munich, Germany

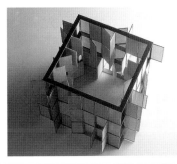

Central Market
Nancy, France

Bercy–Tolbiac Footbridge
Paris, France

*Temple of Mitra
Naples, Italy

Topkapi Exhibition in Versailles
Versailles, France

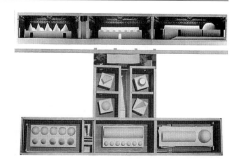

Corsican Maritime Station
Marseille, France

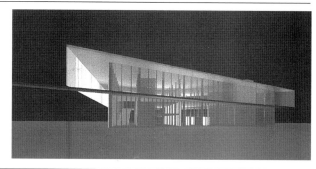

Venice University Institute of Architecture
Venice, Italy

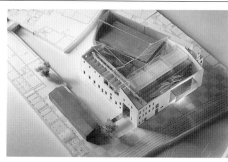

***Montigalà Sports Complex**
Badalona, Spain

Urban Developments Linked to the Tramway
Bordeaux, France

***Lehrter Bahnhof Tower**
Berlin, Germany

P O Box
Villeurbanne, France
Exhibition project

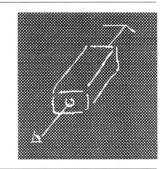

Exhibition Park and Service Centre
Bâle, Switzerland

1997 **Development of the Place Roger Salengro**
Dunkerque, France

Bank for the Foundation WANAS
Stockholm, Sweden

*Central Media Library
Vénissieux, France

*Hotels in the Antilles
Guadeloupe – Martinique – Guyana

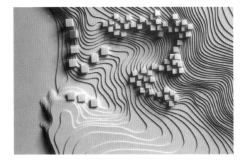

*APLIX Factory
Le Cellier, Nantes, France

Costantini Museum
Buenos Aires, Argentina

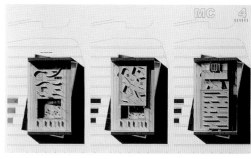

Olympic Village
Kitzbühel, Austria

Development of the BLEG Grounds
Berlin, Germany

Centre for Political Security
Geneva, Switzerland

*The Museum of Modern Art
New York, USA

French Embassy
Berlin, Germany

Refurbishment and Extension du Cargo
Grenoble, France

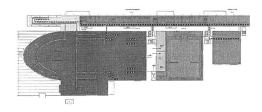

Haute-Savoie Departmental Archives
Annecy, France

Town Plan
Marly-le-Roi, France

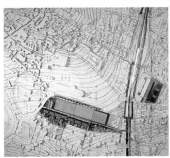

Refurbishment of the Montparnasse Tower Site
Paris, France

1996 **FEDEX European Centre**
Aéroport Charles-de-Gaulle, Roissy, France

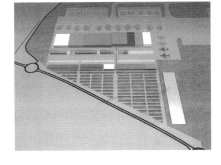

Concert and Theater Hall
Château-Gontier, France

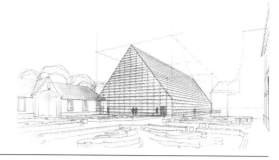

International Airport
Dortmund, Germany

Ministry of Foreign Affairs
Berlin, Germany

Development of the Heart of the "Vieux Pays"
Tremblay-en-France, France

*Kansai-Kan Library
Kyoto, Japan

Archive Centre
Rheims, France

*Great Extension of the European Union Court of Justice
Kirchberg Plateau, Luxembourg

*Kolonihavehus Installation
Copenhagen, Denmark

Urban Lighting Structures
Paris, France

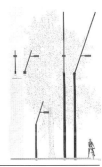

*Innsbruck Town Hall
Innsbruck, Austria

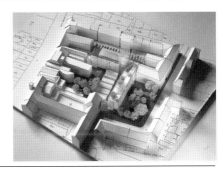

ELEC'96 Central Stand
Villepinte Exhibition Park, France

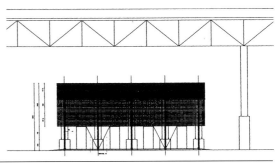

1995

*Installation Project for Francis Giacobetti's Work HYMN
Paris, France

Expansion of Municipal Stadium
Marseille, France

Place des Nations
Geneva, Switzerland

***Pre-landscaping and Redevelopment
of the UNIMETAL Site**
Caen, France

**Aménagement of Storkowerstrasse near
the Olympic Velodrome and Swimming Pool**
Berlin, Germany

Brive–Montauban Autoroute
France

Metro Entrance
Parizerplatz, Berlin, Germany

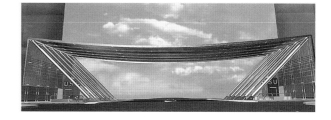

Ministry of Culture Buildings, Rue Saint-Honoré
Paris, France

***The Great Greenhouse,
Cité des Sciences et de l'Industrie**
Paris, France

Furniture for the Bibliothèque nationale de France
Paris, France

Very High Tension Pylon
France

1994 **International Harbour Terminal**
Yokohama, Japan

***Headquarters of Bayerische
Hypotheken und Wechselbank**
Munich, Germany

Aménagement of l'Ile Saint-Anne
Nantes, France

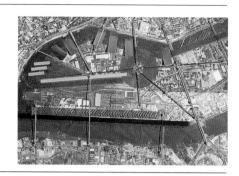

Sparkasse Bank
Salzburg, Austria

Glass House
Düsseldorf, Germany

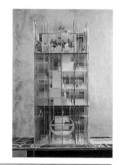

Stand for the German Cinema Museums at SIME
Paris, France

*Private Villa
Bretagne, France

1993   ***The Grand Stadium**
Melun-Sénart, France

New Installations for the Zoological Park
Vincennes, France

***Book Technology Centre**
Bussy-Saint-Georges, France

Fondation Erol Aksoy
Istanbul, Turkey

Stand TECHNAL at BATIMAT
Paris, France

Neptune Water Purification Plant
Nantes–Petite Californie, France

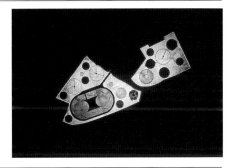

Wilhelm Gallery
Potsdam, Germany

1992

SULZER areal
Wintherthur, Switzerland

*Olympic Velodrome and Swimming Pool
Berlin, Germany

Development of the Place d'Youville
Montréal, Canada

Development of the Two Banks of the Garonne
Bordeaux, France

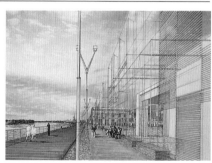

*Lu Jia Zui Business District
Shanghai–Pu Dong, China

World Centre for Peace
Verdun, France

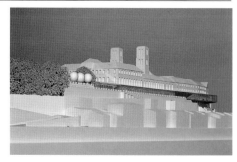

School of Mines
Nantes, France

Domrémy Carpark
Paris, France

1991   **House for the Meuse Department**
Marne-la-Vallée, France

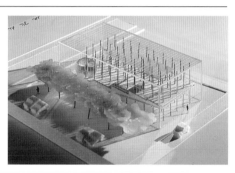

Alliance Française
Singapore

Business District
Créteil, France

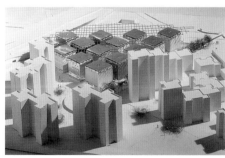

Galerie Denise René
Paris, France

Technopole CITIS
Hérouville, France

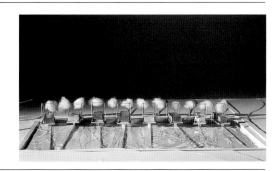

1990 **Niffer Canal Reach**
Mulhouse, Rhin–Rhône, France

Zone d'Activité Concertée Tolbiac–Massena
Paris, France

1989 ***Bibliothèque nationale de France**
Paris, France

***IRSID, Usinor-Sacilor Conference Centre**
Saint-Germain-en-Laye, France

Workshops of the Decaux Factory
Plaisir, France

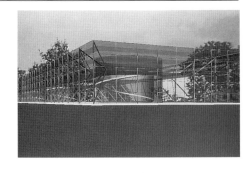

*Archives for the Mayenne District in Laval
Laval, France

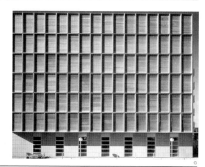

Axis of the Earth, Piotr Kowalski
Marne-la-Vallée, France

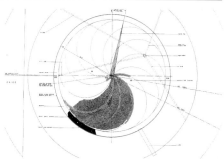

Porte d'Italie Offices
Paris, France

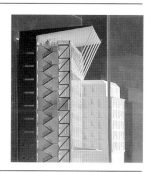

Angers Exhibition Centre
Angers, France

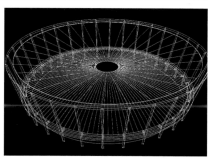

*Ecole Nationale des Ponts et Chaussées,
(ENPC–ENSG)
Marne-la-Vallée, France

Saint-Jacques Hospital
Clermont-Ferrand, France

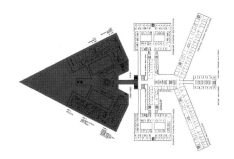

IFMA
(Institut Français de Mécanique Avancée)
Aubière (Clermont-Ferrand) , France

ISMRA
(Institut des Sciences de la Matière et du Rayonnement)
Caen, France

"Les Balcons du Canal" Housing Development
Paris, France

Technical College
Clermont-Ferrand, France

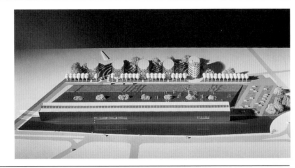

European Palace of the Rights of Man
Strasbourg, France

Port of Boulogne
Boulogne-sur-mer, France

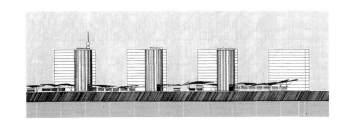

Social Headquarters of Technip
Rueil-Malmaison, France

Zone d'Activité Concertée of the White Cross
Bussy-Saint-Georges, France

1988 **Offices of CGI**
Villepinte, France

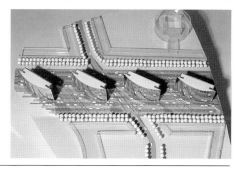

Maternity Hospital Centre
Albertville, France

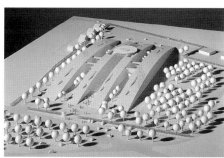

School of Mines
Douai, France

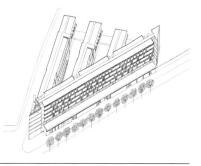

Gymnasium
Sèvres, France

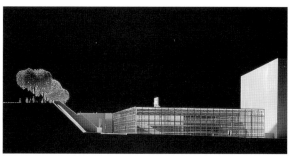

Percy Army Hospital
Clamart, France

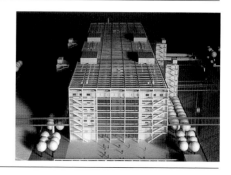

Meuse Departmental Building
Bar-le-Duc, France

Hysope
Paris, France

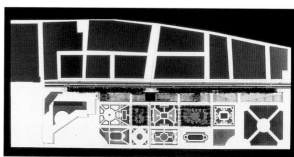

"Le Louis Lumière" Housing Development
Saint-Quentin-en-Yvelines, France

College of Biotechnologies
Nancy, France

Pont Charles de Gaulle
Paris, France

*Headquarters of Canal+ TV Channel
Paris, France

Headquarters of the Newspaper *Le Monde*
Paris, France

Ski Jump
Courchevel, France

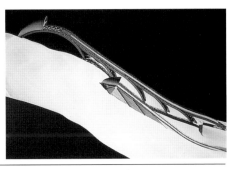

Francis Le Basser Stadium
Laval, France

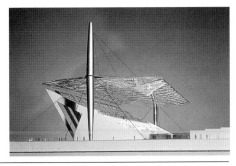

Methanol Plant
Angers, France

1987   **Development of the Loire Banks**
Rézé-les-Nantes, France

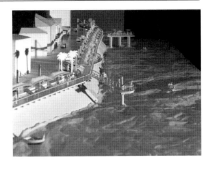

Halle Saint-Louis
Lorient, France

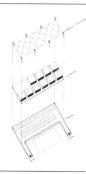

Mas House
Spain

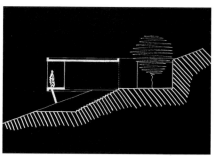

*Water Purification Plant for S.A.G.E.P.
Ivry-sur-Seine, France

1986 **STAG Publicity Agency**
Paris, France

CFDT–Bolivard
Paris, France

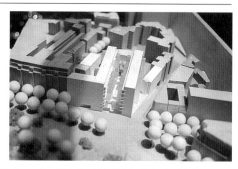

Chartreuse Matalis
France

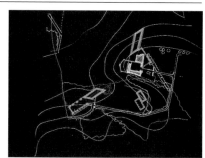

*Hôtel Industriel Jean-Baptiste Berlier
Paris, France

"Les Cap Horniers" Housing Development
Rézé-les-Nantes, France

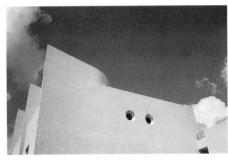

Européan Synchrotron
Grenoble, France

Zone d'Activité Concertée Chevaleret
Paris, France

1985

**Mission du Conseil Architecture, Urbanisme
et Environnement Loire-Atlantique**
Corcoue-sur-Logne, France

University of Angers
Angers, France

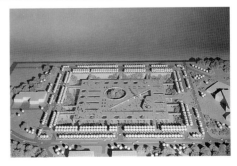

Factory I2L
Marseille, France

SOMEREP–FRESCHARD Factory
Marne-la-Vallée, France

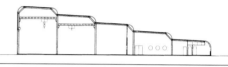

1984

Distribution Centre for SEITA
Marne-la-Vallée, secteur 3, France

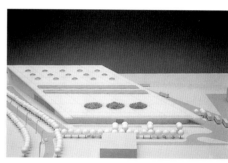

***University for Electrical and Electronic
Engineering**
Marne-la-Vallée, France

Command Post of the Périphérique
Paris, France

1983   **National Laboratory of Health**
Montpellier, France

1982

Three Communal Houses, PAN XII
Rézé-les-Nantes, France

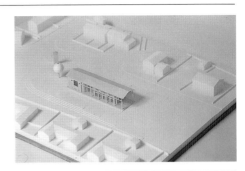

1981

SOMELOIR SCET Factory
Châteaudun, France

Acknowledgments

The many specialist, services and structural consultants who have been involved in the major projects of the practice are too numerous to mention, but gratitude and acknowledgement in particular is owed to Gaëlle Lauriot-Prévost, who has been responsible for the organisation and creative control of a great part of the office's design work.

A special thank-you to Gaëlle Lauriot-Prévost and Natalie Plagaro Cowee for their perseverance and work in collaboration with the team of The Images Publishing Group to achieve the highest standards for this publication. I would also like to thank Frederic Migayrou, author of the Monograph's Introduction, for his generosity.

Dominique Perrault

Index

Bold page numbers refer to projects included in
Selected and Current Works